D1207577

NEBRASKA

KANSAS

COLORADO

ROCKY

Big Blue R.

Miss. River

Smoky Hill River

Kansas River

Quivira

Hutchinson

Kingman

Medicine Lodge

Arkansas River

Sangre de
Cristo
Mountains

Beaver City

Santa Fe

Pecos

Tiguex

NEW

MEXICO

MOUNTAINS

Canadian River

OKLAHOMA

TEXAS

Rio Grande

MEXICO

GULF OF
MEXICO

To Compostella

FRANCISCO CORONADO
AND THE SEVEN CITIES OF GOLD

ALSO BY RONALD SYME

ILLUSTRATED BY WILLIAM STOBBS
ALEXANDER MACKENZIE, CANADIAN EXPLORER
BALBOA, FINDER OF THE PACIFIC
CAPTAIN COOK, PACIFIC EXPLORER
CARTIER, FINDER OF THE ST. LAWRENCE
CHAMPLAIN OF THE ST. LAWRENCE
COLUMBUS, FINDER OF THE NEW WORLD
CORTES OF MEXICO
DE SOTO, FINDER OF THE MISSISSIPPI
FIRST MAN TO CROSS AMERICA
FRANCIS DRAKE, SAILOR OF THE UNKNOWN SEAS
FRANCISCO PIZARRO, FINDER OF PERU
HENRY HUDSON
JOHN SMITH OF VIRGINIA
LA SALLE OF THE MISSISSIPPI
MAGELLAN, FIRST AROUND THE WORLD
THE MAN WHO DISCOVERED THE AMAZON
ON FOOT TO THE ARCTIC, THE STORY
 OF SAMUEL HEARNE
SIR HENRY MORGAN, BUCCANEER
VASCO DA GAMA, SAILOR TOWARD THE SUNRISE
WALTER RALEIGH

ILLUSTRATED BY RALPH RAY
BAY OF THE NORTH

ILLUSTRATED BY JACQUELINE TOMES
AFRICAN TRAVELER, THE STORY OF MARY KINGSLEY
NIGERIAN PIONEER, THE STORY OF MARY SLESSOR

RONALD SYME

illustrated by
WILLIAM STOBBS

William Morrow and Company

New York 1965

FRANCISCO CORONADO
AND THE SEVEN CITIES OF GOLD

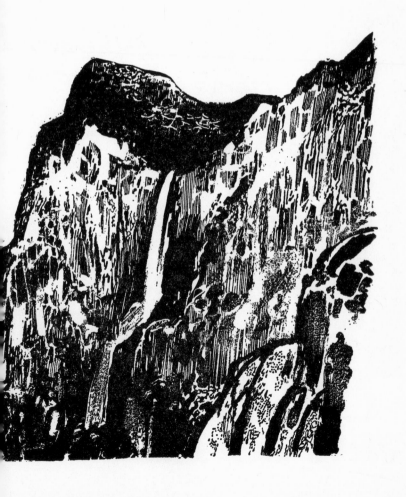

Second Printing, March 1967

Library of Congress Catalog Card Number 65-15336

CONTENTS

CHAPTER
ONE

THE LOST EXPLORERS

The dignified and haughty assembly called the High Council of New Spain, or Mexico, was meeting in solemn session. In an ornate and well-padded chair at the head of the long and paper-littered table sat His Excellency Don Antonio de Mendoza, the newly appointed gov-

9

ernor of Mexico. By virtue of his high position Don Mendoza was the most powerful official in the New World. Members of the High Council, imposing in rich velvet doublets, lace collars, and jewelry, took care always to address him in the most courteous and flowery language.

Though His Excellency's own manners were equally stilted and ceremonious, he was by no means in an amiable mood. In fact on that particular day he disliked the very sight of his worthy colleagues.

It was the early summer of the year 1537. The weather in newly built Mexico City was already unpleasantly hot. Through the open windows of the spacious Council Chamber a dry wind entered in puffs. No coolness came with it, merely an odor of damp earth. In the open sunbaked square outside the building, stolid and half-naked Indian slaves sprinkled the bare earth with water in an effort to keep down the dust.

It was Don Mendoza's second summer in Mexico, and his health was enduring the season no better than it had the first one. Prickly heat tormented his sensitive skin. Recently a burning fever—brought, although Don Mendoza did not know it, by mosquitoes that haunted the city's stagnant wells—had afflicted him for almost a whole month. The fever had only been cured by repeated draughts of a strange and shockingly bitter Indian medicine that the Spanish residents called Jesuits' bark and we now know as quinine. Finally His Excellency had suffered a number of gastric complaints, caused—although once again Don Mendoza did not know it—by too many highly spiced dishes, pastries, and sugary preserves.

There were matters other than his health to worry Don Mendoza. He appeared to be listening with polite attention to the various matters being dealt with by the High Council. But inwardly he was moodily reflecting that not a single member had yet touched on the most

important and pressing matter of all. Since
Francisco Pizarro's discovery of the enormously
wealthy country of Peru in 1532, almost every
Spaniard in Mexico was eager to seek his fortune in that newer, gold-filled land of the
Incas. Too many of them were leaving Mexico
as fast as they could. There was already a danger that Mexico would soon become a stagnant
and backward country with a decreasing population of Spanish settlers. Once the conquered
Aztecs realized how few Spaniards were left,
the faint chance existed that they might unite
to drive out the hated invaders.

What was needed, brooded His Excellency,
was another near miraculous discovery of some
rich and vast Indian city somewhere in Mexico
—or in the unknown countries that lay to the
north of it. The golden loot from its temples
would doubtless be sufficient to pay for the
new cathedral in Mexico City, the building of
new roads, and all the gunpowder and other

equipment needed to blast open new silver lodes in the mountains of Mexico itself.

Unless some such discovery was made within the next year or so, Don Mendoza pondered fretfully, there was a serious risk that the coffers of his government would be sadly empty. In that event the Spanish king in far-off Seville would certainly not be pleased. Such displeasure might even cost Don Mendoza his handsomely paid appointment.

A discreet knocking on the double doors of the Council Chamber caused Don Mendoza to abandon his morose and depressing thoughts. A sallow-faced, heavily built little man with a neatly trimmed black beard and flourishing mustache, he sat up irritably in his vast chair. "See who it is," he said sharply, when his mild-mannered secretary glanced at him in an enquiring manner.

The secretary arose from his chair and tiptoed across the spacious chamber. For a few moments he remained in the doorway listening to the whispered message of an official who wore the royal red-and-yellow livery of Spain. Presently the secretary returned to Don Mendoza's chair.

"A matter of some importance, Your Excellency," he murmured. "Four men, who declare they have a marvelous story to relate of their wanderings, desire audience of Your Excellency. I understand that three of them are of distinguished and well-known families in Spain."

The gloomy expression on Don Mendoza's face lessened. It was odd that these tidings should come at the very moment when he was thinking of possible discoveries in nearby countries. "Bid them enter," he commanded, delighted with the excuse to interrupt the Council meeting.

The first three men who appeared were supposed to be Spaniards. But their features had been so burned and darkened by sun and wind that they could just as easily have been taken for nomadic Indians. The clothes they wore were of reasonable quality, although they fitted none too well and gave the impression of being borrowed. Yet the self-possessed manner in which these strangers walked across the carpeted floor and made their elegant bows to His Excellency marked them at once as true gentlemen, or hidalgos.

The fourth man was a tall, wide-shouldered, and handsome Negro. He was dressed in a modest white shirt and cheap linen knee breeches, and he bore himself erect and fearlessly.

One by one the first three strangers stepped forward, made a second and deeper bow, and announced their name. Don Mendoza noticed with increasing curiosity that all three spoke formal Spanish with a slight hesitation and with almost a trace of foreign accent. It was as if they had grown unaccustomed to the soft and lisping speech of royal Castile.

The tall, lean man with the strange gray eyes, who appeared to be the leader, declared himself to be Alvar Nuñez Cabeza de Vaca, of the town of Jerez in Spain. He added that he had formerly held the position of civil governor of a province in Spain.

The second hidalgo, swarthy-faced and of slender but wiry build, was Alonso del Castillo. He had the air of a professional soldier even before he announced, with excusable pride, that he was one of the officers who had accompanied Balboa on his famous march across the Isthmus of Panama in the year 1514.

The third and youngest man, who appeared less robust than his two fellow countrymen, gave his name as Andres Dorantes. By his elegant speech and manner it was plain that he, too, was of distinguished family.

De Vaca then presented their Negro com-

panion. His name was Esteban, he hailed from West Africa, and he had lived in Spain for a number of years. "I commend him to your notice, sire," added de Vaca. "Although he is but a humble slave, he has proved himself a good sailor and a man of great courage and endurance."

A former high official of the Spanish Government, thought Don Mendoza, a veteran professional soldier, and a young man of very good family. Naturally they were gentlemen of honor. It was unlikely that any tale such men told would be false, and in their story might lie some clue as to the whereabouts of the wealth so badly needed to strengthen Mexico's ailing finances.

His Excellency glanced at the members along both sides of the table. "Our meeting is adjourned forthwith, *señores,*" he declared, "so that we can hear this report. Let chairs be brought on which our guests may be seated.

The Negro, Esteban, has permission to withdraw."

"Our story is a long one, Your Excellency," said de Vaca, as he seated himself. "You and the Council may grow weary before we have made an end to it."

The governor made a polite gesture. "It is of no matter. The business on hand is not pressing, and I assure you that my own interest is greatly aroused."

During the next three hours, while the sun rose to its noonday zenith and the breeze from the open windows became oppressively sultry, Cabeza de Vaca told his story.

He and his three companions had come to Florida with the powerful and well-provided expedition of a Spanish adventurer named Pánfilo de Narváez. The purpose of this expedition was to discover the fabulous city of Cibola. This kingdom was believed to lie somewhere in the interior of North America. The ships had reached Florida in 1528 and disembarked four hundred men.

All had gone well for a short time. Then the Indians began to harry the Spaniards as they marched north along the west coast. Soon one misfortune followed another. They lost contact with the ships that had brought them to Florida from Cuba, and the Indian attacks became fiercer. In January, 1529, Narváez and his surviving men reached Apalachee Bay on the northwest coast of Florida. At that point the Spaniards came to the conclusion that to advance any farther by land was impossible. The whole countryside was aroused and hostile toward the white invaders.

"Our Captain General therefore decided to build a number of barges," said de Vaca. "In these craft he proposed that we should sail westward along the unknown coast until we came to the province of Tampico in Mexico. We knew that our fellow countrymen lived in that province and, therefore, we would be able to obtain assistance."

Five barges were built by men who lacked both skilled knowledge and the necessary tools. The vessels were launched toward the end of January, 1529. In April the barge in which de Vaca was sailing with some forty companions, including Castillo, Dorantes, and Esteban the Negro, was wrecked on the coast near the site of the future city of Galveston, Texas. Only four men survived that midnight disaster. They were the ones who now sat before the High Council of Mexico.

"For the next eight years we wandered westward across the unknown continent," continued de Vaca. "We knew that our only chance of returning to civilization lay in reaching Mexico. We crossed unnamed mountains and rivers, and all but died of thirst in many deserts. Sometimes the Indian tribes treated us as honored guests, but other tribes enslaved us and treated us most brutally. With God's help we survived until we met a group of Spaniards on the west coast of Mexico. Their leader, Diego de Alcatraz, provided us with an escort. In that manner we proceeded to Mexico City and now appear before Your Excellency to submit our report."

There was a thoughtful silence in the Council Chamber as de Vaca stopped speaking. His story was so strange that the listeners scarce knew where to begin asking questions. It was clear, however, that these four men had accomplished a tremendous and unheard-of journey. They had crossed the entire width of the American continent, a country of which the Spaniards in the New World knew absolutely nothing. They had survived an experience that had probably killed four hundred other men.

"Tell me," said Don Mendoza eagerly, "what you learned about this famous city of Cibola. It is a matter that interests me greatly. Did you reach it? Does it contain as much gold as the Indians declare? In which direction does it lie?"

De Vaca hesitated. Alonso del Castillo made answer for him. "We did not ask the Indians for information about it, Your Excellency," he said bluntly. "Our only idea was to reach Mexico. True, we heard reports and rumors and fanciful descriptions. But I for one, sire, do not believe that the legendary city of Cibola actually exists."

Don Mendoza frowned. This answer was not the one he had hoped to receive. Was it possible, he wondered, that these three men might be withholding secret information from him? Perhaps they knew more than they pretended and were hoping to gain vast profit for themselves by keeping quiet.

During the days that followed the reply made by Castillo to Don Mendoza became a great topic of conversation in Mexico City.

Spaniards reminded one another of the manner in which Cortes had stumbled upon the unbelievably wealthy kingdom of the Aztecs. Francisco Pizarro, that illiterate soldier, had discovered the even richer empire of the Incas in Peru. Surely there could not be only two such wealthy countries in the New World? Cibola must exist somewhere in North America.

Haunted by greedy thoughts of sudden wealth, the Spaniards in New Spain swiftly came to the conclusion that Alonso del Castillo, the veteran soldier, was wrong. Perhaps his party had kept too far to the south and so missed reaching Cibola. Perhaps they *had* seen the wonderful city, but were saying nothing about it.

De Vaca was questioned time after time by Don Mendoza and the High Council. He steadfastly refused to admit that he had any definite information regarding the city. In the end, however, he perhaps grew tired of his questioners' greedy faces and their endless suspicions. He gradually admitted that he had heard many rumors regarding Cibola. Having learned several of the Indian dialects, he had no difficulty in understanding what the natives said.

"It is true that some of the Indians we met wore crude gold ornaments and what might have been precious stones," he declared. "I do not know whence such things came nor did I ask. Yes, some of the Indians mentioned Cibola to me. They said it actually consisted of seven towns. They declared that those places were rich and heavily populated. We did not see any of those seven cities, therefore I cannot say that any of them actually exist."

These tired statements by de Vaca increased the cupidity of the Spaniards in Mexico. Cibola *did* exist, they declared. The Indians to the north wore much gold and jewelry, and de

Vaca himself had said that they were wealthy people. Castillo was merely a cunning fox, who was keeping his mouth shut. Dorantes appeared still somewhat shocked and dazed by his past adventures and therefore better left alone. Esteban the Negro was merely ignored by these avaricious busybodies.

While all the excitement over Cibola was daily reaching fresh heights, there appeared in Mexico City a French missionary named Brother Marcos. He was a stalwart priest who had been present at the conquest of Peru. It was alleged that he had walked all the way from Peru to Mexico City, a distance of 4500 miles through equatorial swamps and across high ranges of mountains.

Although perhaps well-meaning, Brother Marcos seems to have been a gullible fellow. He was much too ready to believe everything he heard about the seven cities of Cibola. Having learned that Don Mendoza proposed to send a small party in the supposed direction of Cibola, Marcos immediately offered to act as its leader. The governor accepted his offer and ordered Esteban to serve as guide.

Amidst the greatest excitement and enthusiasm, Brother Marcos set off in March, 1539. He was accompanied by another missionary named Brother Onorato, Esteban, and a number of friendly Indians.

CHAPTER
TWO

**BROTHER
MARCOS**

The party headed northwestward until it reached the Spanish province of Culiacán on the Pacific Coast. It was the most northerly outpost of the Spanish dominions in Mexico. Once they left Culiacán, the explorers would be entirely on their own.

29

Moving northward from one Indian village to another, paddling or swimming across rivers, climbing high sierras, and crossing wide tracts of waterless desert, these sandaled monks in their somber gray robes finally came to Arizona. They were the first Europeans to reach a point so far north. By this time they had covered some 2000 miles from Mexico City.

Meanwhile, Esteban was scouting through the country several days' journey in advance of the rest of the party. During the eight years he had spent roving across America, the Negro had become thoroughly Indian in his ways. He could track wild animals, scent water at a great distance, and handle a powerful bow with skill. But his return to civilization, after spending so long in the wilds, had merely brought fresh slavery to Esteban. He certainly found this bondage irritating after the utter freedom he had known.

What actually happened to Esteban remains

a mystery. He disappeared somewhere in southeast Arizona or perhaps New Mexico. Brother Marcos was told by some Indians that the Negro had been killed. It was also rumored among the tribes that Esteban had arranged to have this report of his death sent back to the missionary in order to prevent any search for him being made. At any rate, he simply vanished. Perhaps he preferred a free and savage existence to slavery under a Spanish master.

From the reports Esteban had sent back, and from what he had heard for himself, Brother Marcos grew even more optimistic. He was finally sure that the seven cities of Cibola lay only a few days' journey ahead of him. In his official report he wrote:

> I did not dare to penetrate any further into this region. I believed it to be more important to return to Mexico with the tidings I had obtained concerning the seven towns and the kingdoms in which they are situated.

The entire Spanish population of Mexico City, from the governor down, waited in tense expectancy while Brother Marcos, later, finished penning this report. Don Mendoza eagerly read every word the missionary had written. At last His Excellency thought he had the proof of what he already believed. Brother Marcos wrote:

The natives are as familiar with Cibola as we Spanish are with Madrid. . . . Cibola is a vast town, very heavily populated and with a great many streets and boulevards. In some parts of it there are enormous houses which have seven stories. At certain times of the year the chiefs meet in one or other of these houses. The walls of these buildings are made of white limestone. The doors are usually colored a deep turquoise blue. The six other cities which comprise the kingdom of Cibola are all constructed in the same manner, but a number of them are larger than Cibola itself. It is said that the largest city of all is named Ahacus.

Carrying on this glowing report, Brother Marcos wrote:

I had brought with me several samples of different kinds of metals by which I hoped to identify those I found in this new country. I showed these metals to the Indians. They took the gold and told me that the inhabitants of Cibola had bowls of the same material, and that they wore nose rings and earrings of it. Also that they had tiny golden scoops which they used to brush the sweat off their faces when they were working. . . . Elsewhere I learned that the doors of the houses in Cibola are ornamented with turquoise-studded designs. These precious stones are very common in the city.

Brother Onorato, who had accompanied Brother Marcos, was unable to take part in the compilation of this report. He was a very sick man. His health and endurance had proved unequal to the ordeal of plodding across sizzling deserts and climbing in the thin cold air of the high sierras.

To give Brother Marcos his due, he was undoubtedly a brave and hardy explorer. But like many early explorers, he was too willing to believe everything he was told, provided it coincided with his own theories. In his own mind he wanted the legends of Cibola to be true, and so he twisted every scrap of evidence until it seemed to indicate that Cibola really did exist. After all, he was one of those who would stand to benefit most if the cities were as rich as he predicted. A grateful Spain would certainly reward his services with a gratifying promotion within the Church.

Few people in Mexico City paused to reflect on the strange fact that the only three Spaniards who were at all familiar with the interior of North America—de Vaca, Castillo, and Dorantes—spoke much less optimistically about the existence of Cibola. Castillo, the outspoken captain, continued to express his opinion that the city did not exist at all. De Vaca and Dorantes, far from showing any interest in the whole question, went off back to Spain. Soon afterward Castillo left Mexico City and sailed for Peru. Not one of the four adventurers now remained in Mexico.

But by this time Don Mendoza was completely convinced that Cibola actually existed. Any doubts he may once have had were speedily banished after reading Brother Marcos's enthusiastic report.

"An expedition must be organized forthwith," His Excellency announced grandly. "Spain's glittering empire in Mexico must be extended northward to include this rich new jewel of the kingdom of Cibola."

There was no need for Don Mendoza to spoil this noble sentiment by adding that the cash from Cibola would come in handy for paying the salaries of his administration. Everyone knew that the government's money chests were growing somewhat light. Only one question was left unanswered. Who was to be the leader?

There were plenty of dashing cavaliers in Mexico. They were men, of high courage and empty pockets, who would be only too glad to accept such an honorable position. But, as Don Mendoza was well aware, such men were difficult to handle when the fighting was over and their pockets full. They became ambitious and inclined to set themselves up as independent and rebellious rulers in whatever country they had seized. Even at the present time, the tiresome and hot-headed Pizarro brothers in Peru were proving an unpleasant problem to the Spanish government.

Thus while wellborn Spanish gentlemen squabbled and intrigued and eyed each other jealously, Don Mendoza, who frequently found his countrymen tiresome company, brooded alone in the private suite of his official palace. Pen in hand, he carefully crossed off one distinguished name after another. This man was too stubborn; that man was exceedingly vain; Señor So-and-So was of somewhat doubtful character.

At last only one name remained. His Excellency pondered over it for a long time. The man was a newcomer to Mexico. He came of an old and highly respected family, who owned much of the town of Salamanca in Spain. Only thirty years old, he had recently married an extremely pretty heiress, Beatrice Alonso d'Estrada. She was supposed to have the royal blood of Spain in her veins. Shortly after the wedding had taken place, her husband had been awarded the governorship of the province of Culiacán on the western coast of Mexico. The young couple were now in residence there at the capital town of San Miguel.

This new provincial governor was an excellent horseman and said to be proficient in the use of weapons. His father was still serving as a high officer of state under King Charles of Spain. It was rumored that his son held some strange views which, if frankly expressed, might get him into trouble one day. But on the other hand, reflected Don Mendoza, a young man, of good family, who was newly married to a rich and attractive young wife and who held the coveted governorship of a Mexican province was not likely to be troublesome. He would stand to lose too much by displaying any rebellious spirit.

Don Mendoza nodded approvingly. He laid down his pen and leaned back in his chair. He had selected the man who would lead the expedition to Cibola.

The man was Francisco Vasquez de Coronado.

THE GENTLEMEN ADVENTURERS

The famous Spanish University of Salamanca had given Coronado a fine education. He could speak and read both Greek and Latin, was a skilled poet, and had studied civil law. Once it had seemed sure that he would grow up to inherit the family estates and lead the pleasant but idle life of a well-to-do Spanish gentleman.

But when Francisco Coronado was thirteen years old, the news of the Spanish conquest of Mexico reached Spain. Soon afterward, transatlantic galleons unloaded in Spanish ports the rich treasures seized from the Aztecs. From then on the youth of the country were eager to sail for the New World and seek adventure, and perhaps fortune, for themselves. Coronado, who was apparently not at all keen on the idea, allowed himself to be influenced by his friends. He pushed aside his books, acquired a horse, a sword, and a suit of armor, and sailed for Mexico in 1535. He was then twenty-six years old.

Coronado did not have the build or appearance of a swaggering Spanish conqueror. He was of medium height, quiet-spoken, and had open, attractive features. From a distant ancestor, who had migrated to Spain from Brittany in France, he had interited a fair complexion and brown hair. This coloring distinguished him greatly from his darker-skinned, black-bearded countrymen. A Spanish historian who knew Coronado personally wrote:

His training in law and years of study had given him a wise head and a nimble tongue. Few of his friends cared to argue foolishly with him, for his quick wit and ready replies often made an opponent appear exceedingly stupid.

The years he spent at the university had given Coronado startling beliefs and ideas that were centuries ahead of his time. He did not approve of burning Indians at the stake or of chasing them for sport with extremely savage dogs. He preferred to study their language and customs and to make friends with them. Soon after he became governor of Culiacán, trouble arose between him and an overzealous Spanish missionary. The priest wished to set fire to an Indian village, because its superstitious inhabitants had pulled down a large cross that the missionary had erected. The dispute was finally referred to Don Mendoza for settlement.

"To burn a man's home," Coronado said frankly to His Excellency, "is perhaps scarcely the best way to teach him to love and respect a God of whom he may never have heard."

Coronado won that particular argument, and the Indian village was left unharmed. Don Cristobal de Pineda de Coronado, his father, was a trusted friend of King Charles. His Excellency Don Mendoza was anxious to prevent any word of the foolish squabble reaching the king's ears. There was a risk that the king might agree with Coronado.

News of his selection as leader of the expedition to find Cibola brought little pleasure to Coronado. He was reluctant to leave his comfortable home at San Miguel, where he had begun to surround himself with books and to make a study of the Aztec language. But to refuse the high honor offered him was impossible.

A refusal would tarnish his name and reputation.

History reveals that right from the start Coronado was not a firm believer in the existence of Cibola. He was inclined to doubt the accuracy of Brother Marcos's reports. He regarded the information that the missionary had obtained from local Indians as vague and unsatisfactory. Yet no such doubts had entered the heads of those adventurers who were eager to join the expedition. There was merely general approval that Coronado, who was popular throughout Mexico, had been chosen as leader.

It seems likely that Coronado never wrote an account of his expedition. Certainly no such account exists today. A few of his letters on the subject are all that remain. Brittle, age-yellowed reports of Spanish explorers such as Pizarro, Balboa, and Cortes still repose in the great libraries of Spain. But a report by Coronado is not among them. Later historians were thus inclined to overlook Coronado's tremendous contribution toward European knowledge of the interior of North America.

Pedro Casteñada de Nagera is scarcely mentioned in Spanish historical writings, but this almost unknown man did leave a complete record of the entire expedition. All that is known about him is that he was one of the officers who went with Coronado into North America. Apparently he kept a diary of the day-to-day adventures which befell the expedition. Twenty years later, while living in Culiacán, Casteñada wrote that full story for publication. He was obviously a well-educated and intelligent man, accustomed to expressing himself on paper.

Casteñada died before his manuscript reached the printing press. For nearly 300 years after his death the 157 pages that contained his story lay in a dusty library in Mexico. They were finally discovered and published in the year 1838 by a distinguished French geographer named Ternaux-Compans.

Once Coronado had been chosen as leader, plans for the expedition went swiftly ahead in Mexico City. Most of the recruits were young and penniless hidalgos. They had nothing to lose by going, and they hoped they might have a lot to gain. Each of these men was expected to supply his own horse and weapons. Within several weeks 250 of them, along with Brother Marcos, had been selected to accompany Coronado.

Matters were different when it came to finding recruits among the foot soldiers. There was much less enthusiasm in that quarter. For one thing, the men knew very well that when it came to fighting, the Indians always attacked them first and left the cavalry as much alone as possible. Moreover, they were not keen on marching for hundreds, and perhaps thousands, of miles across unknown mountains and deserts in the faint hope of being lucky enough to fill their pockets with gold.

Only seventy foot soldiers could be found to

join the expedition. There were also 300 friendly Indians and a vast horde of cooks, bearers, and personal servants. The total strength of the force amounted to 1000 persons.

"Which is enough," said Coronado sharply, "to found a new region of the Spanish empire overseas."

He was in favor of a smaller and more lightly burdened force, which could make better time in its daily marches. This view was unpopular among the Spanish gentlemen. They all insisted on being accompanied by at least one personal servant and a packhorse on which to carry a valise and other belongings. They also demanded that vast numbers of cattle, sheep, and pigs be brought along to ensure that there would be plenty of fresh food daily.

Coronado became irritable. "We are not going to found a colony, gentlemen," he declared impatiently. "Nor are we farmers in search of homesteads. I fear the day may come when you will regret all the equipment and fine clothes and fancy wines you insist upon taking along."

"Nor are we ragged adventurers, *señor*, to carry what little we own on our back," retorted Lopez de Samaniego, the officer in charge of baggage.

"I would rather wear a shirt for a week and walk with a knapsack on my back than be dressed in fine velvet and have to drive sheep across a desert," said Coronado. "You are over-burdening yourselves. Some way must be found by which our people can lessen their load."

He went to see Don Mendoza on the matter. The governor suggested that the superfluous baggage should be loaded into two ships. These vessels would sail along the west coast of Mexico and keep abreast of the army as it marched northward. It was a risky and doubtful plan. The coast was almost unknown and no charts of it yet existed. But Coronado agreed with the governor's suggestion.

In the early spring of 1540 the little army marched out of Mexico City and headed for the town of Campostella near the west coast. During that 400-mile journey, Coronado's prophecy began to prove accurate. The Spanish soldiers and even the Indians were inexpert in securing loads on packhorses and mules. The animals were fat and lazy and reluctant to travel at all. The wake of the army soon could be charted by packages and bundles that had fallen unnoticed or been craftily thrown aside by an irritable attendant in charge of a mount. More than one expensive suit of armor and valise containing fine clothing was lost in this manner. Grumbling loudly, the haughty cavaliers forgot their lofty pride. They began to load the packhorses themselves and to ride beside these ambling mounts throughout the day.

A great many of the cattle and pigs either strayed or were stolen in the high and lonely hills of central Mexico. The sheep, which suf-

fered greatly, were soon all gone. It was a dusty and hungry army that finally trailed into Campostella and ravenously set about filling empty stomachs.

Don Mendoza in person followed the army across Mexico to Campostella. He was wise enough to travel separately with a number of gentlemen and a well-served baggage train, which included plenty of provisions and comfortable tents. Presumably His Excellency did not intend to endure discomfort on the road.

Having arrived at Campostella, Don Mendoza ordered Coronado's small army to pass before him in review. Casteñada, who had already begun his diary, noted that this inspection went off very well indeed.

First came the young cavaliers mounted on splendid horses. They wore a coat of mail polished to shine like that of their leader, whose gilded armor with its brilliant trappings was to bring him many a hard blow from Indian warriors a few months later. Then appeared the stolid and well-disciplined ranks of the seventy infantrymen. They wore a padded cotton jerkin or plain steel breastplates. On their head was a helmet made of steel or tough bull hide. They carried heavy crossbows and also a few clumsy firearms known as arquebuses. These weapons weighed twenty pounds, took a minute to load, and had a range of sixty or seventy yards. The ponderous barrel had to be rested on a firing stick planted in the ground. Some of these foot soldiers, however, were armed with nothing more than a sword and shield.

When the review was over, Don Mendoza set off on his leisurely return journey to Mexico City. Coronado and his army began the 350-mile northward march to the province of Culiacán of which he was the governor. The two vessels that had been ordered to accompany the expedition were already anchored off the coast. Now there was no reluctance among the cavaliers to place their superfluous baggage aboard the ships. As Coronado had predicted, they were becoming content to travel with nothing more than well-filled saddlebags.

Culiacán was the last outpost of Spanish territory in Mexico. Once the army marched out of it, they would pass through country that was still in the hands of the Indian tribes.

Coronado ordered the advance from San Miguel, the capital, to begin in the autumn of 1540. By then the strangeness of the unfamiliar countryside and the mild hardships they had already suffered had caused a sharp decline in the enthusiasm of the hidalgos. They were beginning to have second thoughts about Cibola. Two of the foot soldiers deserted and made their escape.

"If the good Brother Marcos had seen the wealth of Cibola with his own eyes," declared a twenty-four-year-old cavalier named Tristan d'Arellano, "he would surely spend more time hastening our progress and less on his daily devotions!"

This comment reached the ears of the missionary himself. He acted hurriedly to check such growing doubts and pessimism. "Have no fear for the future," he told the assembled men at prayers the following morning. "I will show the way into a prosperous country from which none of you will return empty-handed."

The two ships accompanying the army were under the command of a certain Pedro d'Alarçon. This impatient gentleman soon began to fret at the slow advance Coronado's army was making in its daily marches. He gave orders for the *Saint Pierre* and *Sainte Catherine* to sail more swiftly in order to reconnoiter the unknown coast that lay ahead.

Three days later the seamen observed low white shores and sandy hillsides lying across their northerly course. Without knowing it, they had been sailing up the Gulf of California and had now reached its northern end.

Discovering the mouth of the Colorado River, d'Alarçon decided to go exploring in his ships' boats. He spent fifteen days ascending the river and made friends with a great number of Indians on the way. Apparently he became so interested in the journey that he gave little thought to Coronado marching along the coast behind him.

D'Alarçon was a brave officer, but possibly he lacked common sense and discipline. Suddenly remembering his orders, he buried a number of letters for Coronado under the roots of a large tree growing near the beach. In one of these letters he casually stated that as his vessels could go no farther north, he intended to return to the port of Altata Salinas, in Culiacán, whence he had sailed.

During his homeward voyage d'Alarçon kept a watch for Coronado's men near the coast, but he failed to sight them. This was not surprising. The expedition had swung inland and was now following the upper course of the Sonora River into the mountains. The *Saint Pierre* and *Sainte Catherine* merrily continued back to their home port, taking with them all the baggage the hidalgos had stored in the holds.

"In this manner," wrote Casteñada in his diary, "a great many possessions were lost—at least to the rightful owners—forever."

Meanwhile, the expedition was having a difficult passage across the aching deserts of northern Mexico. Casteñada wrote:

> The discouragement of the men increased with the difficulties of the way. Our horses were tired and the slow progress became even slower. Some of the horses and Indian carriers fell down and died. Corn was almost gone, and as a result of eating certain fruits and herbs which they found, a Spanish soldier and some of the servants were poisoned so badly that they died. There were thirty leagues (seventy-five miles) of traveling before we reached the borders of an inhabited country where we found fresh grass and many nut and mulberry trees.

This fertile area lay some five hundred miles north of Culiacán. It was here that young Tristan d'Arellano, who was acting as second-in-command to Coronado, decided that he had had enough of the expedition for the time being. Remaining behind, he built a small fort and barracks on the slopes of a pleasant valley and garrisoned the place with a number of sick or faint-hearted soldiers. He named the district Señora, and it bears the name Sonora today. Much later, d'Arellano rejoined Coronado and continued with the expedition.

Shortly after leaving the coast and beginning to follow the Sonora River, the army was forced to halt while fresh provisions were sought in the countryside. At the head of one small party of horsemen, Lopez de Samaniego rode into an Indian village. The narrow street winding among the mud huts was deserted and the doors were closed. Wishing to see around him more clearly, de Samaniego raised a hand and lifted the visor of his steel helmet. A dark and slender arrow flashed from somewhere in the shadows of the houses. De Samaniego fell dead from his horse. The shaft had struck him in the middle of his forehead.

When the army again rested for a few days in order to allow their horses to graze, an officer named Melchior Diaz set off with twenty-five men to follow the Sonora River down to the sea.

They traveled in a southwesterly direction and soon came to a province where the Indians were of a tremendous height. They lived in curious underground huts from which only the thatched roofs projected above the ground. These natives were of such great strength that they could carry on their head loads exceeding three or four hundred pounds. One of them, on seeing six of our men struggling to lift a heavy piece of timber, picked it up by himself and carried it without trouble to the fire and placed it gently on the flames.

When these Indians travel during the winter, they wear little or no clothing, but carry a flaming torch in one hand by means of which they warm themselves. The tallest Spaniard among us was only breast high to these giant warriors.

These Indians told Diaz that they had sighted two strange vessels off the nearby coast and that a boat from one of them had rowed to the shore. They guided Diaz to the spot, and there he located the tree under which Captain d'Alarçon had hidden his letters.

Diaz and his party rejoined Coronado along the upper reaches of the Sonora River. The expedition soon came to the headwaters of this river. Now they were in high country and surrounded by snow-capped mountains 10,000 feet in height. The cold was intense. The Spaniards made camp at four o'clock every afternoon, and from then until dark they were busy felling pine trees for their campfires. A number of the Indians from the warm central plains of Mexico were unable to stand the cold. When the freezing winds of midnight crept down from the mountain peaks and stars were brilliant in the frozen sky, these wretched servants died even as they lay beside their blazing fires. In this manner ended the year 1540.

For fifteen days Coronado led his men through the forbidding sierras. Finally they crossed the future boundary into Arizona at the spot where the Coronado National Memorial stands today.

Huddled in his blankets, the tireless Casteñada continued to write in his diary by firelight every evening. But on this high plateau of seemingly endless mountains, he found it impossible to keep an accurate record of the route they followed. There were no Indian villages, no well-worn trails, no mighty rivers to serve as landmarks. The Spaniards had only primitive navigational instruments. They measured distances by counting the paces they took in each day's march.

All that is known of Coronado's route is that he passed through southeast Arizona and so came to the gentler Black Range mountains of southwest New Mexico. Tall, handsome Californian pine trees grew numerously in the red soil.

We also found a kind of oak tree which was covered with a species of sweet acorn, the kernel of which was as sweet-tasting as sugar (pecan tree). Water cress grew in a number of the springs, also, and we saw many wild rose trees, also the herb which we call pennyroyal, also wild marjoram. In the rivers were barbel and perch very much like those in Spanish streams. Roving through the hills were fawn-colored mountain lions.

Scattered among these mountains were a few small Indian villages whose inhabitants seemed to live by nothing but hunting. They spoke an unknown language, but when eagerly asked by the Spaniards as to the whereabouts of Cibola, they unfailingly pointed to the north or northeast.

This fact delighted the optimistic Brother Marcos. "This whole countryside is exactly as Esteban described it," he said. "We are on the very threshold of the great kingdom of Cibola!"

Many of the Spaniards were now becoming much less optimistic than the missionary. They gazed at the bare hillsides and rocky valleys and the primitive mud-and-stone huts in which the Indians lived. It was impossible to imagine a gold-filled, glittering city in this dreary wilderness of a countryside.

On across the hills marched the Spaniards, perspiring under the increasing heat of the sun. They had long since forgotten the early days when they ate beef and mutton and pork at almost every meal. The crossbowmen were becoming expert at hunting the twenty-pound

turkeys that roosted on the pine trees in great numbers. (The arquebuses were too inaccurate to knock them down.) The cavaliers, who had once been accustomed to dainty and well-spiced dishes, now scrambled eagerly along the muddy banks of the streams as they searched for fish to eat. During these last few days of the march to Cibola, Brother Marcos, that well-meaning priest, kept urging Coronado to cover greater distances every day.

On July 7, 1541, after traveling nearly 1500 miles from Campostella, the weary Spaniards reached the crest of a mountain ridge. And there, in the valley below, they saw the first of the promised seven cities of Cibola.

CHAPTER
FOUR

**THE
SEVEN
CITIES**

Coronado had never expected much, but even he could not believe his eyes. The more hopeful Spaniards, including those who were prepared to reach a city smaller than the almost fabulous Mexico discovered by Cortes, literally burst into tears. Casteñada himself, writing

68

twenty years afterward, still sharply recalls the dismay felt by himself and his companions.

It was a little unattractive village, looking as if it has been crumpled up together. There are mansions in New Spain (Mexico) which make a better appearance at a distance. It was a village of about two hundred warriors. The mud-walled cottages are three and four stories high, but they are very small and have only a few rooms. Such were the angry words that some of our men hurled at Brother Marcos that I pray God may have protected him from them.

The Spaniards were gazing at the first Indian pueblo they had seen. It was a town of unusual appearance; a single vast house constructed on three sides of a court. The outer walls were usually built of thin slabs of gray sandstone. There were several crooked stories, which were divided by separating mud walls into long rows of small apartments. The stories rose in uneven terraces, each narrower than the one beneath. They were accessible only by narrow outside ladders, and the whole building was thus well-protected against an enemy. As many as 1500 Indians sometimes lived in the 400 or 500 rooms that the larger pueblos of New Mexico contained.

"I have seen honeycombs that were better built," murmured Coronado, when he recovered from the shock of his first glance at Cibola. "Yonder building looks as if it were made of brown sugar that has melted in the sun and rain!"

But none of his companions smiled at this jest. In grim and furious silence they tramped on down the slope until they came to a halt a hundred yards from the pueblo.

All the available Zuñi Indian warriors were drawn up in line across the rocky path that led to their queer village. They carried primitive bows and wooden spears with bone-tipped

points. "Go back!" they said to the Spanish interpreters. "We cannot feed so many of you."

The Spaniards' disappointment sharpened into cruelty. Without awaiting a command from Coronado, they surged forward to attack.

The Indians fled quickly back into the pueblo. They hid themselves in doorways, windows, and on the narrow balconies that ran along the front of each terrace. From these places they fired arrows, hurled rocks, and tipped over the ladders up which the Spanish troops were ascending.

Coronado reached the outer walls of the pueblo, shouting to his angry men to draw off from the attack. A heavy stone struck his helmet with such force that the steel was badly dented and he himself fell unconscious from his horse. Three Indians promptly dashed out from the shadows to stab him with bone-bladed daggers. Two other Spanish cavaliers, Garci-Lopez de Cardenas and Hernando de Alvarado, drove off the Indians and dragged Coronado to a place of safety.

The attack on the pueblo lasted for an hour. Gradually the Spaniards reached the upper floors. The entire population then contrived to escape from the pueblo and fled toward an extensive pine forest in the distance.

Coronado, who had recovered consciousness by that time, watched them depart. "There go five hundred people, every one of whom is a bad ambassador for us," he murmured. "We will not have many friends in this country."

Brother Marcos was already discovering for himself what it was like to be friendless. He decided to return to Mexico, "fearing," as Casteñada noted, "to remain any longer with the army lest the men should do him an injury." He departed with two cavaliers and some Indians as escort, and so disappears from the pages of history.

The expedition remained in the deserted

pueblo for a few days. Small parties of mounted Spaniards rode out in all directions from Cibola. They proceeded to the other villages, which, viewed from a safe distance, appeared no larger or richer than Cibola. None of the Spaniards were attacked, because, as Coronado had predicted:

A rumor had reached the Indian tribes that Cibola had been captured by a very ferocious nation who rode large animals which devoured men. As the Indians had never seen horses, this news made them very afraid.

One of these nearby villages was a place named Tusayan. It was located close to the site of the modern town of San Marcial on the Rio Grande. There the Spaniards first heard of the strange spot known today as the Grand Canyon. When this news was relayed to Coronado, he selected Garci-Lopez de Cardenas, who had saved him from being stabbed to death, to go in search of this place, accompanied by twelve men.

Cardenas set off on this 400-mile trip to the northwest. With his party went six horses laden with supplies of food and water. The Spaniards had heard that much of the route lay across a desert that would take them twenty days to traverse.

It was now late summer of the year 1541, but a white covering of snow still lay on the sierras. The men often gazed longingly at this remote snow as they wearily made their way across the hot wastes of the Painted Desert. Yet the clear, starlit nights were pleasantly cold. The men huddled round their mesquite fires and grumbled when the predawn cold penetrated the single blanket that covered them.

When the twenty days were past they reached the river of which they had heard. Its banks were so elevated that our men got the strange impression that they were several miles above the earth.

The countryside was covered with low stunted pines and very exposed to the north. The cold at night was so great that it was almost impossible to tolerate. For three days our men wandered among the surrounding hills, always searching vainly for some route by which they could go down to the river. Owing to the enormous depth of this great valley, the river itself appeared to be no more than some six feet in width, yet the Indians declared it to be actually well over a mile.

At the end of the third day Cardenas came to a spot where descent seemed possible. Captain Melgosa, Juan Galeras, and another soldier, who were the lightest men present, volunteered to make the attempt. Next morning they began climbing down the bank until they were lost to view of those who remained behind. About four o'clock in the afternoon they returned and said they had been unable to accomplish the whole journey. They had managed to cover about a third of the way, and even then the river had begun to appear so much larger that it was not difficult to believe what the Indians had said about its actual width. Captain Melgosa added that a number of rocks on the floor of the valley, which from above seemed no higher than a man, were actually higher than the belfrey of the cathedral in Seville.

Lack of water prevented Cardenas from going any farther, and the aching silence of the immense wilderness was beginning to have an ill effect on his men's nerves. Turning their back on the Colorado River, they began the return journey across the Painted Desert. Grand Canyon was to be left undisturbed in the loneliness of northern Arizona for more than another two centuries.

At the expedition's headquarters in the Cibola pueblo, Coronado thought carefully about the future. He had fulfilled his orders and led his men to the so-called Seven Cities. Strictly speaking, his task was done. He would be perfectly justified in ordering a return march to Mexico. There is little doubt that he desired to go back. According to Casteñada, Coronado often spoke in most wistful terms of his wife and their pleasant home in San Miguel.

But one thought prevented Coronado from issuing the order. "Our king and His Excellency Don Mendoza do not receive tidings of failure gladly," he remarked to some of his friends. "To return empty-handed to Mexico would not bring luster to our name or reputation. If we go forward we may chance upon the wealth that we have failed to find in Cibola."

It was during this period of doubt and hesitation that the cavalier Hernando de Alvarado chanced to meet an Indian whose words raised the hopes of the gloomy and pessimistic expedition. Alvarado had gone with another party of men to examine a village named Acuco. It was probably located somewhere close to the

site of the present day Gila Cliff Dwellings National Monument.

This place was very strong, because it was up
on a towering plateau whose sides were so steep
and so elevated that only a very good musket
could throw a ball to the top of it. There was only
one means of access to this village. This was by
means of a handmade ladder which commenced at
the foot of the plateau and led upward to the village. The ladder was comfortably wide at its base
and upward for the first two hundred rungs. But
then the ladder narrowed considerably for the next
hundred rungs. And finally there came a gap of
eighteen feet, which could only be traversed by
placing one's hands and feet in holes cut in the
rock face. No army could be strong enough to
capture this village. Acuco had a population of
about two hundred warriors and their families.
They were robbers feared by the entire surrounding countryside. On the top of the plateau they
had sufficient space to sow and store a large
amount of corn and for cisterns to collect snow and

water. These Indians gave our men presents of a large number of turkeys with very big wattles, much bread, tanned deerskins, fir cones (which made very convenient fuel), cornmeal, and corn.

Having prudently made friends with these robber Indians instead of picking the usual Spanish quarrel with them, Alvarado was told that lying about three hundred miles to the northeast were several important Indian villages. The largest of them, standing on the site of the New Mexico town of Bernalillo, was named Tiguex.

Alvarado was a tough and somewhat brutal young man; he was also quite fearless. Without hesitation he set off to inspect Tiguex. As he had less than a dozen men with him, the Indians of this village refrained from making any attack on his little party.

Alvarado then rode on another sixty miles and so reached the enormous pueblo of Cicuye, where the town of Pecos is today. The Indians there appear to have been the forefathers of the Apache nation. They gave Alvarado a friendly welcome, and he spent several days in their pueblo.

During this time Alvarado met an Indian who declared he was a native of the country somewhat to the north of Florida. The Spaniards gave him the nickname of Turk, because he was said to resemble the people of that nation.

Through a Mexican Indian interpreter, who had now grown familiar with the language of these people, Turk gave Alvarado some wonderfully fascinating information. "If it is gold you seek," he said, "you should come to my country. Here in the plains that surround Cicuye the buffalo provides the only wealth these poor Indians possess. But in *my* country gold and silver are more plentiful than buffalo hides and deerskins among these people."

Alvarado hastened back to Cibola, taking

Turk with him. On the way he met Coronado, who had begun to advance across the Black Range mountains and had, in fact, almost reached Tiguex. The expedition made camp on the outskirts of that city, and Alvarado hurriedly brought Turk into Coronado's presence.

Once again the Indian related his dazzling stories of wealth. "The name of my native province," he said, "is Quivira. Our herds of buffalo, deer, turkey, and many other kinds of wild creatures are infinitely more numerous than on this dreary mountain plateau where you now find yourselves. A river (the Missouri), which is five miles wide, runs through Quivira. In its waters are fish as big as horses. Along this great river sail the splendid canoes of our princes. Each vessel has more than twenty paddlers to a side. They are fitted with masts and sails. In the stern there is a raised poop where, under a silken awning, reposes the prince to whom the vessel belongs. The prow of these great canoes is usually adorned with a great eagle modeled in gold."

"A question," interrupted Coronado. "You say the metal is gold. Are you sure it is not copper or some other inferior substance?"

Turk smiled. "I am very well acquainted with gold," he declared loftily. "In every household in Quivira there are dishes made of gold, which we call *acochis* in our own language. The metal is so common that I could not make a mistake about it."

One of the cavaliers immediately handed him a gold ring, a piece of copper, and a small brass medallion. After examining all three articles in a careful manner, Turk held up the ring. "This is *acochis*," he said.

Coronado was still not satisfied. "How does it happen," he enquired, "that you yourself do not wear any gold or silver ornaments?"

"I had a number of such ornaments, but they were taken from me when I was captured by the people of Cicuye," Turk replied unhesitatingly.

"We will check on the whereabouts of those ornaments," replied Coronado. "How did you come to be taken prisoner?"

"It was my own fault," said Turk. "Ever since I was a boy I have been fond of wandering. I left my home in Quivira in order to visit the countries which lay farther to the west."

Coronado paused. The cavaliers had been eagerly listening to this conversation. From the avaricious expression on their faces it was clear that they believed every word that Turk said. But Coronado was not convinced. He still remembered the wonderful tales told by Brother Marcos.

"Don Alvarado," he said, "I must ask you to return to Cicuye. Try to recover the gold ornaments that this man says were taken from him. Or at least find out whether he was actually wearing any such ornaments."

When Alvarado reached that village, the inhabitants again received him in a friendly manner. But they declared in the most fervent manner that they knew nothing of any gold bracelets, and they insisted that Turk was a very great liar. Alvarado thereupon invited their chief, an elderly man named Bigotes, to his tent and there made him a prisoner in chains. The Indians furiously declared that Alvarado had revealed his true character and was a man who broke his word. They attacked the Spaniards with their bows and arrows, whereupon Alvarado and his company retreated with his prisoner whom he took back to Tigeux.

By their stupid methods the Spaniards had once again made fresh enemies. This incident was to have serious results before very long.

CHAPTER
FIVE

BATTLE
OF THE
PUEBLO

Winter of the year 1541 was closing down over the countryside. A bitter wind swept across the sierras and whistled round the closed doors and shuttered windows of the pueblo near Tiguex in which the Spaniards had installed themselves. Inside the little rooms the troops crouched around smoky fires.

93

As the cold grew more intense, a number of the soldiers began seizing the warm buffalo robes worn by the Indians. These thefts increased the hostility between the two races. The Indians were already in an ill humor, because they had been evicted from this particular pueblo in order to make room for Coronado's men.

Trouble began one sharp and frosty morning in late November. One of the friendly Indians who had accompanied the expedition from Mexico City suddenly raced into the pueblo. He was wounded and very frightened. "The Apaches are in arms!" he shouted. "They have killed my comrade and now they are driving away your horses."

Cardenas, the discoverer of the Grand Canyon, was hastily ordered to take troops to the scene of the trouble. "Try to pacify them," said Coronado. "Avoid killing if possible. There is enough trouble for us in the countryside already."

Cardenas arrived just as a band of Indians were leading out some of the horses from the warm stables that had been prepared for them. The Spaniards were greeted with showers of arrows and screeching war cries. In a fury at being discovered, the Indians proceeded to kill the horses that they had attempted to steal. They then raced back to their own village.

Cardenas and his men tried to follow them. They were driven back by arrows and stones hurled down on their heads from the rooftops. One soldier was struck by an arrow, which penetrated his leather jerkin and protruded for several inches from his back. Many others were wounded by flying stones and shafts.

This minor skirmish gradually developed into a general battle, which went on all day and night. When darkness came the warriors lurked in narrow alleys and attacked advancing Spaniards with knives and tomahawks. Captain Diego Gutierrez had his steel helmet slashed open by a tremendous blow from one of these weapons, and he was lucky to be knocked senseless instead of killed.

Next morning the Spaniards grew alarmed at the number of casualties they had suffered. They began trying to smoke the Indians out of the pueblo with great bonfires. This plan proved successful, and the singed and half-suffocated warriors surrendered before noon.

Without informing Coronado of his intentions, Cardenas, who was one of the senior officers, ordered that two hundred of the Indian prisoners should be burned at the stake. While the firewood was being prepared the prisoners were kept under guard in a large tent. They suddenly realized the fate intended for them. Seizing wooden billets, cooking pots, stools, and other improvised weapons, they attacked their guards. Several more Spaniards were killed in this sudden fight, and many of the Indians met their death at the hands of other soldiers who hastened to the spot. But a number of the warriors managed to escape by hiding in dark corners of the village until nightfall. They then managed to flee from the neighborhood of Tiguex.

In an angry mood Coronado sent for Don Cardenas. What was said between them remained a secret, but certainly from then on Garci-Lopez behaved in a more moderate manner toward the Indians. What alarmed Coronado was that two soldiers named Pedro Almaden and Lopez Henares had died of minor arrow wounds. It was probably accidental tetanus infection, but the terrified Spaniards believed otherwise.

"Poison!" one muttered. "The Indians are starting to use poisoned arrows against us."

Coronado was horrified by this belief. Choosing a mild and prudent hidalgo, whose name Casteñada omits from his diary, he ordered him to visit all the nearest villages and try to restore peace between the inhabitants and the expedition.

The Indians were in no mood for smoking

the pipe of peace. Those in the smaller villages disappeared as soon as the party of horsemen appeared in sight. Fast-flying arrows and leveled spears awaited the Spaniards in the larger villages. Then, utterly without warning, the entire population of the neighboring town of Tiguex burst into fierce rebellion.

This latest attack could not have come at a worse time. No way of retreat lay open to the Spaniards across the snow-covered ranges. They were pinned down in their quarters, and there they had to fight or die. Instead of waiting for an attack to be made on the camp, Coronado ordered his troops to seize the pueblo of Tiguex.

Our leader ordered a number of ladders to be made, and we then advanced against the town in good order. As soon as we were close to the walls, we received the order to attack. But the enemy had had ample time in which to prepare their defenses and now they hurled down great showers of heavy stones on our heads. Many of our men were struck by these rocks and knocked senseless. . . . The siege went on for fifty days during which our repeated assaults were driven off. The enemy suffered greatly from thirst; they dug a very deep well inside the village, but without finding water. The walls of this well finally collapsed, burying thirty men who were working inside it.

This grim account of the battle for Tiguex ends with the words:

More than twenty of our men were wounded by arrows and a number of them died. We also lost Francisco de Pobares, a brave gentleman, and Captain Francisco d'Obando was taken prisoner by the Indians and dragged away to their town.

It is easy to imagine the fate that overtook the unfortunate Captain d'Obando at the hands of his Indian captors.

Coronado remained bitterly opposed to this savage warfare between the Indians and his own men. He ordered the attack to cease for an entire day in the hope that the besieged warriors of Tiguex would agree to yield. But the Indians, who apparently trusted Coronado himself, merely sent out their women and children. These unfortunate people were allowed to proceed freely to safety. The warriors themselves remained behind the stout walls of Tiguex.

Fifteen days later the Indians decided to break out of the town. They waited until midnight and then began leaving Tiguex secretly in small parties at a time. An alert Spanish sentry happened to notice some furtive shadows and shouted an alarm. He was swiftly stabbed to death, along with the other men in his picket. The Indians then made a break for it. They plunged fearlessly into the icy waters of the Rio Grande and began swimming across the river.

Our soldiers followed them across the river in boats. On the farther bank they found a number of

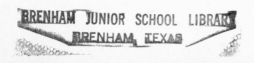

wounded Indians who had collapsed from the cold and loss of blood. On the orders of our general, these natives were cared for and later became servants attached to our camp.

Sick and weary of all this fighting, Coronado suggested to his most senior officers that it might be wiser to return forthwith to Mexico. There seemed no purpose in remaining any longer in this land of bitter hatred and bloodshed.

The cavaliers disagreed with this view. They were enthralled by Turk's vivid descriptions of the opulence of Quivira. They insisted on pressing onward until they reached that part of the country. Coronado realized that an order to retreat would immediately start a mutiny among his own men.

By this time, however, a few of the more levelheaded Spaniards, of whom Casteñada was one, were beginning to share Coronado's suspicions about Turk. A Mexican Indian named Isopete, who had been with the Spaniards since the start of the expedition, insisted that Turk was nothing but a tremendous liar. Bigotes, the captive chieftain, swore that when his warriors had captured Turk they had found no golden ornaments on their prisoner. Finally a Spanish soldier, who had been detailed to keep an eye on Turk, announced his belief that the Indian had evil powers of magic! When asked by Coronado to explain himself, the soldier said:

During the siege on Tiguex I kept Turk closely confined in a hut and allowed no visitors to see him. One day he asked me who were the Spaniards who had been slain during the fighting for Tiguex. I told him that none of our men had been killed recently, whereupon Turk replied, "You lie. The Indians have killed one of your officers and five soldiers." When I made some enquiries I discovered that this was correct; six of our men had indeed been killed. I asked Turk how he knew this, but he only laughed and said, "I don't need anyone to tell me simple things like that."

Whatever Turk might be, the majority of the Spaniards still had much faith in his words. Seeing that they were eager to press on across the country during the approaching summer of 1542, Coronado wisely ordered the release of Bigotes.

This kindly action put the local Indians in a much better humor. They made no fresh attacks as the expedition began to advance from Tiguex across the Sangre de Cristo Mountains toward the great plains, which lay on the other side of this range.

Although the days had now become reasonably mild and sunny, bitter winds swept through the mountains from sunset to dawn. At an elevation of several thousand feet above sea level, the numbed and half-frozen Spaniards were still compelled to wrap themselves in their purloined buffalo robes when they lay down to sleep. More of the Mexican Indians, unaccustomed to the thin cold climate of these altitudes, caught pneumonia and died wretchedly in the passes.

Coronado led the way out of New Mexico and into northern Texas. Then the Spaniards reached the almost illimitable plains.

We now began seeing unbelievable numbers of buffalo. Their leaders stood gazing at us uncertainly and the rest began to flee, falling over one another in the process. They finally reached the edge of a deep ravine into which they fell in such great numbers that they almost filled it. The rest of the herd continued their flight across the dead and crushed bodies of their companions. . . . On that same day a party of Indians told our general that they had traveled some thirty miles without seeing anything but the sky and buffaloes.

The Indians of this region seemed to be living in a higher state of culture than the tribes farther to the west. They called themselves Teyas, wore beautifully sewn leather garments, and had cleanly habits.

After growing utterly weary of the mountains and deserts and empty tracts of country through which they had passed, the Spaniards were delighted with this fresh and pleasant part of the future state of Texas. The wide and peaceful country stretching beneath the summer sky appealed very deeply to some of the humble foot soldiers. A number of them had spent their youth on farms back in Spain. Now they gazed at the rich grass and the tall trees and crumbled the rich, loamy soil between their fingers.

"A man could build a prosperous farm in this country," one of them said. "Corn and fruit and cotton would all grow well. One day, perhaps, after we have found the wealth of Quivira, we will return here to build homesteads and plow the land." Where those soldier farmers stood and dreamed four hundred years ago, the flourishing agricultural and pastoral towns of Texas and Oklahoma stand today.

The hidalgos, who cared little for soil and scenery, were in no mood to linger. Their one idea was to reach Quivira. By this time, however, Coronado was becoming sure that Turk was nothing but an imaginative liar. The local Indians shook their head when questioned about Quivira and declared that they had never heard of such a country.

Finally Coronado called a meeting of his officers. They agreed that Coronado himself, accompanied by thirty cavaliers and six foot soldiers, should go forward in search of the promised Quivira. The rest of the army, under young Tristan d'Arellano, the founder of Sonora, would go back to Tiguex and await the return of the advance party.

Coronado set out with his companions early in June, 1542. With them went Turk, who was

now guarded day and night and slept in chains.

Meanwhile, the army was making preparations for the return to Tiguex. They spent fifteen days slaughtering buffaloes and drying the meat for their return march. During that time, according to Casteñada, they probably killed five hundred of those animals. While out hunting several of the Spaniards lost their way, so flat and featureless was the prairie.

Every evening we called the roll of those who were missing, fired shots, sounded trumpets, and lit great fires. Even so, a number of our soldiers had wandered so far away that they neither saw nor heard anything. A number of them regained the camp by fixing on the point where they had killed a buffalo, and then going in various directions until they recognized the long and shallow ravine in which we had pitched our tents. Other soldiers were brought back to us by wandering parties of Indians, whom they were fortunate enough to meet. A few of the men were intelligent enough to mark the bearing of the sunrise when they set out in the morning, and to observe the approaching sunset in the afternoon when they wished to return to the camp. These observations gave them approximate compass bearings. But the only men who could follow this plan were those who had spent their earlier life at sea.

Four or five of these Spaniards never returned to the camp at all, and no one ever learned what had happened to them. During this same period several horses also strayed and were not recovered. These lost animals were the first of the great herds of broncos, or cayuse, which roamed the prairies in later centuries.

With his army left far behind, Coronado continued to push forward across the burning plains of what was later to become known as Kansas, the Sunflower State. It was now midsummer and the noonday heat was becoming unbearable, especially for the six foot soldiers, who, beside being burdened with their heavy weapons, were still wearing a thick padded jacket and a cumbersome helmet. These men in particular rejoiced when Coronado reduced the length of the daily march to fifteen miles, much of which was covered in the cool interval between dawn and sunrise. Whenever possible, camp for the night was made beside some river in which the men refreshed their weary, dusty, and sun-scorched bodies.

In this manner Coronado covered a distance of four hundred miles and reached the heart of Kansas without meeting trouble of any kind. One evening early in July his party came to a peaceful little Indian encampment. Coronado's description of the natives he found there has been preserved in one of his letters.

These Indians travel from day to day in company with great herds of buffaloes. They eat the raw flesh and drink the blood of the animals they kill. They remove and dress the skins in a most wonderfully clever manner and use them for making handsome clothing for both men and women. They have little field tents made of the hides of the buffaloes, tanned and greased and very well made. These people also possess a great many dogs, which they load for the daily journey with tents and poles and other belongings. They are the finest-built Indians of any tribe I have come across in the Indies.

Unlike his companions, Coronado always made a point of treating the various Indian tribes in a kindly and courteous manner. Now, accompanied by Isopete, his most trusted guide, he approached the camp.

"Tell them," he said to Isopete, "that we are friends who are seeking for a rich and famous country named Quivira. It is a country in which there is both gold and silver."

The Indians stared at Isopete in wonderment as soon as he had translated this remark. "We have not heard of gold, and of silver we know but little," their chief replied. "Yet the country in which you stand at the present moment is called Quivira by all our people."

CHAPTER SIX

THE COUNTRY OF QUIVIRA

After an angry and disturbed night, Coronado ordered Turk to be brought in front of him the following morning.

"Why did you lie?" he demanded. "What gave you the idea of telling us that the country of Quivira was filled with gold and silver? And where is the vast and stately river of which you spoke?"

Confronted in this stern manner, Turk made a forthright confession. "The river you will come to if you march still farther to the east," he declared. "The Indians of Cicuye begged me to contrive some trick that would cause you to become lost in the plains. They said that if only your horses died of hunger it would be easy enough to kill you all when you returned on foot through their country, because by that time you would be both hungry and exhausted. In that way the Indians would revenge themselves for all the miseries your men brought to them. I agreed to the plan because I knew that none of you were skilled hunters and that you could not live on corn alone. I saw that all your people were crazy for gold, so I invented my story about the wealth of Quivira. Now I have told the truth and am ready to die."

Casteñada wrote:

Our people executed Turk forthwith. Apart from his treachery in the past, we feared that he might give the Indians of Quivira some idea of the weakness of our entire expedition and of ways and means by which we might be attacked and overcome. Turk's death delighted Isopete, for the two had always hated one another and Turk had constantly abused Isopete and told us many times that he was a liar.

The Indians of this country certainly had neither gold nor silver and knew almost nothing about either metal. The chief wore on his chest a mere copper ornament of which he was extremely proud.

Once again there was no reason for Coronado to proceed any farther. He had already ventured seven hundred miles beyond his original destination at Cibola in New Mexico. But Coronado did not turn back. Gradually he was being changed by this mighty country of desert and plain, mountain and river, into a tireless explorer.

"We will go forward to find the great river

of which Turk spoke so steadfastly," he said. "One day perhaps it will serve as a highway to the sea for future generations of men."

Past the sites of the yet unborn towns of Medicine Lodge, Kingman, and Hutchinson, the Spaniards rode on across the eternal, trackless plains.

"Should I live to see Mexico again," grumbled a soldier named Alazanas, "I will build a cabin for myself on the top of a mountain. Never again do I wish to live in a country that is as flat and dreary as the ocean on a windless day!"

Coronado overheard his remark. "Be patient," he said smiling. "Moses and his people wandered in the wilderness for forty years. We are merely newcomers!"

They camped for a few days at the spot where the Big Blue River and the Kansas River meet. The men lazed in the warm water, caught barbel with improvised fishing gear, and al-

lowed their horses to crop greedily at the rich herbage along the riverbank.

They were still at this place when Isopete rose to his feet one afternoon and gazed intently at the sky. "There is bad rain coming," he announced. "With it will come the devil wind."

Puzzled by this remark, the Spaniards were still prudent enough to carry various belongings inside their lightly thatched huts. They believed Isopete meant to warn them that a brief squall was approaching.

Before they had finished placing everything under cover, they heard the roar of distant rain sweeping across the prairie. The first tremendous downpour soaked the camp inside a minute. Then hailstones began pelting down, and on seeing their great size the Spaniards crossed themselves nervously and muttered prayers.

Some of the hailstones were the size of hazelnuts, but others were as big as hens' eggs. Hurriedly, the men put on their breastplate and helmet and any other protective garments they could grab. But such was the force of the falling hailstones that many of the Spaniards were knocked down and badly bruised. Some of the terrified horses broke their tether and bolted off across the plain.

The noise of the rain and hail ended abruptly. Peering out of their torn tents and stripped huts, the men saw with horror a funnel-shaped, vapory cloud, which was apparently suspended in the sky a little to the south of them. The air was full of a sulphurous smell, and the strange silence seemed filled with fresh but unknown danger.

"The devil himself is approaching!" muttered a young cavalier named Pedro de Torbar. "Soon he will appear from within that monstrous cloud."

A strange roaring sound was heard in the distance. It grew in intensity and the reek of sulphur became stronger. The inky cloud continued to sweep onward across the prairie at a speed of forty to fifty miles an hour. The terrified Spaniards were appalled to see great cottonwood trees, which were standing in the path of the tornado, snapped off and tossed aloft like fragile weeds. The men threw themselves flat on the ground and their fingers sought desperately for anchorage among the roots of the grass.

A moment later the tornado reached them.

If the diabolical wind had actually passed through the camp, almost certainly some of the men would have been killed. Such is the force of a tornado that cattle, horses, and even houses are torn bodily from the ground and deposited a long distance away.

Coronado and his men were lucky. The base of the twister missed the actual site of the camp. But even as they staggered to their feet, a strange suction knocked them flat again. Then the dreadful din and confusion began to die away. Gradually the flying dust and debris settled back to earth.

If we had been caught by this dreadful tempest when we were on perfectly level ground, we might quite easily have lost all our horses forever. Fortunately, we had pitched our camp in a ravine and were thus given some slight shelter from the full and dreadful force of the wind. But all our tents were badly ripped, helmets were battered and dented, a number of the horses were wounded, and all our crockery and containers were broken. This was a very great misfortune, because it was quite impossible for us to obtain any more in this country.

In spite of all their faults, these undaunted Spaniards possessed endless courage and endurance. Picking themselves up after the tornado had passed and recovering their straying horses one by one, they went on eastward through the beautiful valley of the Kansas River.

They began to meet more and more Indians in this area. Messengers had already sped through the country with the news that white-skinned strangers were approaching. Some of these runners covered distances of eighty and ninety miles between dawn and sunset. Mingled with the Kansas Indians who came to stare at the Spaniards were Osage and Pawnee, many of whom had paddled long distances in birch-bark canoes.

The Spaniards were fascinated by these extraordinarily light and handy craft, which were built with a skill and neatness they had never seen before. They noted that when a canoe contained only one occupant, he always knelt in the stern. It was the custom of these Indians to place a small bunch of grass under the paddler's knees. But what particularly puzzled Coronado was that the Indians paddled only on one side of their canoe yet, with short, two-foot paddles, they managed to maintain a perfectly straight course. The soldier Alazanas, on attempting to paddle one of these canoes in the same manner, merely went around in uncontrollable circles until he finally capsized in the middle of the Kansas River, much to the amusement of the spectators.

The Pawnee Indians showed many signs of friendship toward the Spaniards, over whom Coronado maintained his usual strict discipline. They stated that their supreme chief, whose name was Tatarrax, was anxious to meet the strangers and wanted them to come to his country.

Traveling northward in the company of these big and friendly Indians, Coronado finally came to the chieftain's village of Harahey. It was situated on a point of land that projected into the waters of the Kansas River somewhere near present-day Kansas City.

The surrounding country was the most beautiful the Spaniards had yet reached, being composed of undulating savanna on which grew noble stands of beech, birch, maple, spruce, ash, and walnut. The grass was of the most luxuriant green, and herds of buffalo grazed on it in vast numbers. Among the trees and high undergrowth that covered the little peninsula, the tops of wigwams, with blue smoke curling from the apertures, could be seen only at a close distance.

Chief Tatarrax came striding out to meet Coronado at the head of two hundred finely built warriors. He was an impressive figure.

"It will grieve me when courtesy compels me to dismount," murmured Coronado. "I fear that when I stand beside yonder chieftain, I will appear as a twig beside a tree!"

These Pawnee were the tallest race of Indians, apart from the tribe who lived near the Gulf of California, that the expedition had seen. None of the approaching warriors stood less than six feet in height. Many of them were several inches taller. Chief Tatarrax, however, was a full seven feet. He was about thirty-five years old and a nimble, quick-footed giant. The Spaniards estimated that he must have weighed 250 to 300 pounds. Like all the Pawnee, his head was shaved and painted with great care and considerable artistry. Following the fashion of his tribe, his ears were slit and suspended from them were ornaments of wampum. He was wearing a beautiful deerskin robe, and his leggings were fringed with scalp locks. In one hand Tatarrax held an elaborately carved pipe, in the other a well-balanced tomahawk, from the handle of which dangled more scalp locks.

After the first greetings were exchanged at a distance, Coronado approached the chief on foot. On each of Tatarrax's powerful wrists he placed a heavy brass bangle. Then Father Juan de Padilla, a missionary who was accompanying the party, stepped forward and placed a necklace of colored beads with a pendant cross around the chief's neck. As the missionary stood no more than five feet three inches in height, Tatarrax, with a friendly smile, bent forward to receive the gift.

In this Pawnee village beside the river, Coronado and his men were treated with unending hospitality. They were given well-cooked meals of buffalo meat, corncake, beans, grapes, plums, pumpkins, and a strange but delicious vegetable called a potato, which the Spaniards had never previously seen or tasted.

The war bow used by Tatarrax was an object of great curiosity. It was five feet in length and made from hickory, a tree that grew in great abundance in Quivira. The massive wood was beautifully glossy and elaborately decorated. The bowstring consisted of a strip of carefully twisted deer hide. The arrows, of which Tatarrax carried fifty in his quiver, were slightly more than twenty-four inches in length without a flint-tipped head. The feathers at the neck were fastened in the usual manner of the Pawnee, being secured with a glue made from the hooves of buffalo or deer. They were then bound with fine deer sinew to keep them in place.

On testing this bow, the Spaniards found that they could nearly bend it to its full extent by standing on it and pulling upward on the bowstring with both hands. Juan Alora, a foot soldier who had been a blacksmith in his younger days and was known to be the strongest man in the whole expedition, could just manage to hold the bow in the correct manner and pull the string back less than halfway to his ear. Yet with this same weapon, Tatarrax could easily trace a bird in flight and kill it dead in midair.

While the Spaniards were staying in this village of Harahey, a young Indian whom they had captured and enslaved near Cicuye decided to escape. He had come originally from the Mississippi Basin and belonged to the Natchez tribe, who lived in that region.

Traveling alone for 800 miles southward, this Indian reached his own country early in 1543. There he met 400 destitute and hungry Spaniards, all that remained of the 1000 men who had landed in Florida under Hernando de Soto in 1539.

The Indian astonished these men by speaking to them in a smattering of their own language. He informed them that another Spanish expedition had entered the country far to the north. This news was the first that de Soto's men received of Coronado's presence in North America. Thereafter, the Indian helped the Spaniards with the construction of the clumsy barges that they were building in the hope of sailing to safety in Mexico.

The barges eventually made the voyage to Pánuco on the coast of Mexico, whither they arrived after a terrible journey that lasted fifty-five days. Less than three hundred of the Spaniards survived.

August arrived, and Coronado realized that soon he would be forced to return to his army encamped at Tiguex. But some of the Pawnee who had come to Harahey insisted that the Spaniards should visit with them in their village, which lay to the north.

Moving upstream along the banks of the Missouri River—as noble a river as Turk had declared—Coronado apparently passed close to the site of the future Falls City and thence through the present-day county of Pawnee in Nebraska. At this stage of the journey Coronado's actual route northward from Harahey is puzzling. The country was so featureless that Casteñada found few landmarks to describe.

Casteñada wrote:

> The herds of buffalo were not so numerous in this region. However, the woods and meadows held great quantities of turkeys and the largest kind of deer we had yet seen in this country (wapiti). There were also a great many wolves, bears, wildcats, opos-

sums, and badgers. The country was much more thinly populated, which is surprising in view of its fertility. The various plants and fruits much resembled those of our native Spain.

Father Juan de Padilla took a particular liking to this region between the Big Blue River on the west and the Missouri on the east. Finally he decided to settle there among the Indians.

"These Pawnee are both generous and hospitable," he said to Coronado. "They already have many of the qualities that make good Christians. I ask permission to remain here."

"Should you do so, then I will remain with you," declared a young Portuguese soldier named Campo. "We will provide company for one another in the long and lonely years that lie ahead of us."

Coronado gave Father Padilla and Campo the permission they sought. History records that several years later Campo returned alone to Mexico. He said that Father Padilla had been killed by hostile Indians.

Turning eastward with his Pawnee companions, Coronado arrived back at the Missouri River. So ended his outward journey. Since leaving Campostella in Mexico, he and his companions had traveled more than 3000 miles.

CHAPTER
SEVEN

REVOLT
IN
SONORA

While Coronado was resting on the shores of the Missouri River before starting the return journey, his army had already returned to Tiguex.

Tristan d'Arellano was now in command of the men, who for some reason showed little faith in him. Signs of mutiny were beginning to appear, and there was plenty of evidence that everyone was growing sick of this unprofitable wandering in the wilds.

The coming chill of autumn reminded the Spaniards that their garments, which had already lasted for two years, were rapidly becoming threadbare. Unless warmer clothing could be found, the intense cold of the mountains in winter would become unbearable.

D'Arellano, who certainly lacked Coronado's understanding of human nature, set about overcoming this deficiency in the quickest possible way. Once again he began seizing all the Indian deerskin garments that he could find. This procedure was perfectly satisfactory as far as all the Spaniards were concerned. They ignored the fact that it was certain to stir up fresh trouble with the Indians. What the Spaniards did object to very strongly was that d'Arellano kept the best deerskin garments for himself and

his friends, and gave only those of poorer quality to the rest of the men.

While feelings became bitter in the Spanish camp, the Apache thought up a cunning plan. "The strangers are unskilled hunters," one of the leaders said. "True, they can kill buffaloes with their clumsy and smelly guns, but no man can live for long on buffalo meat alone. From now on we will not supply them with any other kinds of food. We will pull up everything that grows in our vegetable allotments and hide what we have already gathered. We can live well enough on meat and wild-growing plants of which the strangers are ignorant."

The Spaniards suddenly found themselves having to exist on a miserable and insufficient diet of meat and corn. Lack of fresh vegetables gradually brought on an illness called scurvy among them. Then came a fresh danger. Apache warriors, moving stealthily through the darkness, began to kill the sentries.

D'Arellano ordered that the most mutinous soldiers should be placed on guard at all the dangerous points around the camp. The fiery Spanish nature did not take kindly to all these hardships, which totaled up to a thoroughly miserable existence. The grumbling of the men became louder and more venomous.

"The sooner we return to Mexico the better," one muttered. "We came to this country to fill our pockets, not to be roasted by summer heat, frozen by the bitter cold of winter, or murdered in the darkness by prowling savages."

During this gloomy period at Tiguex in the fall of 1542, a party of Mexican Indians suddenly appeared with letters from Don Mendoza, the governor of Mexico. The contents of these letters did nothing to improve d'Arellano's depressed humor.

The governor stated that he was becoming very worried by the long silence of Coronado and his army. He suggested that surely the great cities of Cibola could not have taken so long to locate. Perhaps the wealth from them was already on its way to Mexico City. Very firmly His Excellency indicated his desire to obtain a report from Coronado, which would be brought by the same Mexican Indians.

In this same package of mail was a letter addressed to Don Garci-Lopez de Cardenas, the officer whose cruelty toward the Indians had brought him a severe rebuke from Coronado. The letter stated that his elder brother had died in Spain and that he was now heir to a wealthy estate in his homeland.

"Of which I stand sadly in need," grumbled the cavalier. "My purse was light before I enlisted under our general's banner. The fine horse that I bought in Mexico City is now roving wild on the prairies, its saddle was stolen from my tent, and I shattered my costly Toledo sword in the siege of this town. I shall return to Spain even poorer than when I left."

Cardenas left Tiguex on a borrowed horse and in the company of Mexican Indians.

His companions were astonished to see him ride back into camp some two months later. Now he was accompanied by only one Mexican Indian, who was mounted on a mule. The hidalgo's armor was dented in many places, he had been wounded in the neck, and he was exhausted, dusty, and ravenous with hunger.

"The Indians of Sonora are in revolt," he told the garrison at Tiguex. "They have killed a number of our men with poison arrows. I could not get through the mountains because of lurking ambushes. The Indians who went with me either fled or were killed."

D'Arellano had established his Sonora colony in a village that he named San Hieronimo. Formerly it had been an Indian settlement of mud-walled cabins. The Spaniards merely evicted the Indians, erected a stockade, mounted a few

light guns, built the inevitable chapel, and so turned the place into a lightly defended fort.

Before leaving San Hieronimo in order to rejoin Coronado, who was then marching northward across New Mexico, d'Arellano had chosen the sickly and lazy soldiers to stay behind and act as a garrison. In command of them he placed a small handful of officers who, for one reason or another, were willing to remain in Sonora.

What began to happen as soon as d'Arellano left this settlement would have been easy enough to foretell. The bad elements among the men began to influence others who wished to remain loyal and so grew in numbers with every day that passed. The grumblers declared that they had been betrayed and that they would be abandoned in this distant country.

In some of the villages through which these Spaniards had passed while proceeding northward with Coronado, they came across graceful

Indian vases that had been beautifully decorated with silver. The source of this silver remained unknown at the time. But now the Spaniards left in Sonora located three silver mines, which had been worked by the local Indians for many centuries.

The soldiers suddenly perceived an opportunity to become rich. Using precious gunpowder, which they stole, they blasted the rock and uncovered several fresh seams of precious metal. Greedily they drove the local Indians to work in these mines as slaves. As the ore began to appear, the soldiers became more and more undisciplined. At last their officers had no control left over them.

San Hieronimo stood in a great valley named Suya. On the slopes stood a number of Indian villages. The inhabitants seem to have been normally quiet, simple, and fairly industrious. Their womenfolk were of striking appearance and said by the Spaniards to resemble Moors.

The men were agriculturists and also expert hunters of the wild sheep and goats that lived in the mountains.

These Indians suffered most under the mutinous Spanish soldiers. They were whipped and tortured and made to toil incessantly.

A few of the more intelligent Spaniards in San Hieronimo sensed the gathering storm. "If we wait until the savages fall upon us we will be doomed," one of them said. "It is one thing to die on a Christian battlefield. It is altogether another thing to wait in the darkness not knowing the moment when a poison arrow will inflict its wound to rot our bodies with venom."

"Then let us leave San Hieronimo while there is time," suggested a soldier named Pedro de Avila. "I have become familiar with these mountains during the past months. I know secret paths along the high hills by which we may escape to Culiacán."

One night a small party of these soldiers

crept unnoticed out of San Hieronimo. They traveled for several miles through the hills before the Indians sighted them at dawn. The Spaniards fled along a narrow trail until they reached more open ground. There they halted to make a stand. With crossbows and thunderous arquebuses they managed to keep the Indians at a distance and inflicted casualties upon them. Leaving four of their own men dead, the surviving soldiers reached Culiacán in safety. Their leader, Pedro de Avila, was one of them.

Captain Diego de Alcarraz was the officer in supreme command of the settlement of San Hieronimo. This unfortunate officer discovered with horror that he was now left with not more than eighteen men, some of whom were in poor health. Alcarraz himself was so weak from fever that he could scarcely stand.

Three nights later the Indians crept across a small river that flanked one side of the fort. They entered San Hieronimo without being perceived by the sentries. Shortly before dawn they uttered their war cry and burst out of hiding places. Before the sick or sleeping Spaniards could arm themselves, they were struck down with tomahawk or lance. Captain Alcarraz was killed as he staggered, sword in hand, to the door of his hut.

Only three or four Spaniards survived this massacre. They were the lucky ones who managed to leap onto horses and gallop out of the town. The Indians sacked the settlement, and then returned to the mountains with their booty.

CHAPTER
EIGHT

**RETURN
JOURNEY**

In his camp beside the Missouri River, Coronado was eager to begin his 1000-mile return march to Tiguex. He must cross the plains before bitter winter covered them with snow. The days were still long and sunny, but the windless nights now held a sharp chill that gave warning of approaching autumn.

148

In a pleasant grassy meadow between Falls City, Nebraska, and Atchison, Kansas, Coronado ordered his soldiers to erect a great oak cross. The soldier Juan Alora carved in deep letters on it the following inscription:

Thus far came Francisco Vasquez de Coronado, general of an expedition. God be Praised. August, 1542.

The men busily prepared corn and dried fruit and pemmican as provisions for the homeward journey. Their saddlebags were frayed and torn, but the Indians cleverly stitched new ones made of buffalo hide. These new containers, being better designed than the original ones, were able to hold a large amount of corn. The grain was necessary to the horses to keep them in good condition.

"Do not return overland to the village of Harahey," the Indians suggested to Coronado. "It will be easier to travel along the river."

"Our horses would scarcely fit into your canoes," objected Coronado.

The Indians laughed. "A horse is certainly a heavy animal, but we can make a craft that will carry yours. The work will take three days if you agree to let us have your sharp iron axes."

The Indians went to a nearby stand of forest, which grew almost on the bank of the Missouri. There they felled a number of straight-stemmed beech-trees. Working day and night without ceasing, they hollowed out twenty-foot lengths of the trunks and shaped them into heavy dug-out canoes, each of which had a beam of nearly three feet. They then launched these canoes on the Missouri, moored them in pairs and built twelve-foot-wide wooden platforms between each pair of canoes. These rafts were each capable of carrying three horses. The passengers sat in the canoes at either side of the raft.

On August 12 the Spaniards began their downstream journey. The current, which ran at a good four miles per hour, bore them along swiftly.

Ten miles south of the future town of Atchison they passed an island to which, some two hundred years later, French explorers gave the name of Ile au Vache, or Cow Island.

This island, which I judged to be of one thousand acres in size, was inhabited by great numbers of deer, turkey, bears, and many other kinds of game. At the close of our first day's voyage down the great river, we made camp for the night on the island. The Indians brought in quantities of meat, which we cooked over our fires.

When the rafts pulled in at the mouth of the Kansas River, Isopete, the faithful guide, decided to remain in the country of Chief Tatarrax. The chief supplied Coronado with six of his own men, who could act as guides until the Spaniards were well on the road to Tiguex.

These Indians began leading the way westward. They followed landmarks of their own, and it is impossible to be certain of the route they took. It seems probable, however, that they went along the Smoky Hill River until the majestic peaks of the Rocky Mountains rose glittering above the distant western skyline. At that point they swung southward until they reached the Arkansas River. Crossing this river, the Indians led the way almost due south for another two hundred miles. At the end of that distance the Spaniards sighted familiar landmarks along the stony banks of the Canadian River.

The Indian guides, being lightly armed and of athletic build, set a tremendous pace. They were not content unless they covered distances of twenty-five miles a day. The Spanish foot soldiers, burdened with knapsacks, crossbows, and arquebuses, were always exhausted at the end of these marches.

From the Monday they always looked forward

impatiently to the following Sunday, for it was on that day only that they were allowed to rest in camp. Had they traveled at that speed during the great heat of midsummer, they would soon have used up all their strength. But the nights being now pleasantly cool, and the heat of the sun somewhat abated, our men always felt refreshed by the following morning.

One of these long-suffering Spanish foot soldiers expressed his thoughts in blunter words. "The Indians set a pace," he declared, "which we, not being as fleet of foot as the great mountain goats which we saw daily and envied greatly, found ourselves most exhausted trying to maintain!"

During that 1000-mile journey back to Tiguex, only the Indians in northern Texas gave the Spaniards any trouble. Some of these Comanches had possibly also seen the horses belonging to de Soto's ill-fated expedition. They were certainly the first Indian tribe to realize fully the tremendous use of those animals.

On the first night that camp was made beside the Canadian River two horses disappeared during the darkness. Coronado redoubled his guards, armed them with arquebuses—of which the Indians were needlessly more scared than of the crossbow—and ordered them to fire at the first sight or sound. But the next morning another horse was gone. The animal had been tethered within thirty-five feet of a sentry, but the man had neither seen nor heard anything.

The following night the Spaniards kept great bonfires burning from dusk to dawn. No horse was stolen, but an Indian contrived to slit open the wall of a tent in which a cavalier was sleeping and cunningly remove his saddle. A sentry sighted the man as he flitted away into the darkness. He fired and missed, whereupon the Indian dived into the river with the saddle and made his escape.

Three reluctant hidalgos now discovered for themselves what it was like to keep up with the

Indian guides on foot during the daily marches.

On reaching what Casteñada describes as "that part of the country where the great river (the Canadian) began to divide into a number of tributaries," the Pawnee guides said farewell to the Spaniards and left to return to their own country.

Coronado had now reached eastern New Mexico. Another couple of days brought him within sight of the familiar pueblo at Cicuye. On October 3, 1542, he led his men into the camp at Tiguex. During fifty-two days of marching, the magnificent foot soldiers had covered an average of twenty miles a day, a feat that was seldom bettered in the annals of North American exploration by similarly burdened men.

CHAPTER NINE

BACK TO MEXICO

Far from being discouraged by his unsuccessful journey to Quivira, Coronado was already full of plans for fresh exploration the following year. From being a reluctant leader of the whole expedition he had now fully developed into a tireless explorer.

Our general had decided to spend the winter at this place (Tiguex), and when spring came to advance deeper into the heart of the country, because, he declared, the Indians had already told him that far in the interior was a well-populated region through which flowed many splendid rivers. From the descriptions given him, our general believed that the region in question closely resembled our native Spain in its climate, fruit, and vegetables. Instead of believing that there was no gold to be found in that country, he thought that quantities of it might be located, although the Indians denied it. They were certainly familiar with gold, which, in their own language, they always called *acochis*.

Strangely enough, Coronado was right. Both Utah and Colorado, lying to the north of New Mexico, produce gold and silver in considerable quantities. But then so does New Mexico, although Coronado never knew it.

If Coronado had paused to consider his army more carefully, he might have felt less optimistic about his plans for the following spring.

Most of the men no longer resembled troops in the service of imperial Spain. The red-and-black uniforms of the infantry had long since rotted and been discarded. The fine linen shirts, elegant velvet cloaks, and knee breeches of the cavaliers were going the same way. In increasing numbers the men were donning deer-hide clothing, moccasins, and skin caps. Sun and weather had darkened their already swarthy complexions, thereby increasing their growing likeness to Indians. As they became freer in their choice of costume and more accustomed to the unfettered life of the wilds, their military discipline continued to wane. They were no longer a compact Spanish expedition; they had become a mere rabble of adventurers bound together by the circumstances of their existence and the mutual need for protection.

Undoubtedly, however, Coronado had a sound reason for wishing to prolong his exploration. He still remembered that a valuable discovery would bring him honor, wealth, and distinction. Failure to make any such discovery would result in cold disfavor in Spanish royal circles.

These facts were brought home to Coronado as he sat alone in his mud-walled apartment in the Tiguex pueblo to write to Don Mendoza. D'Arellano had wisely left the task to him. The letter is another of the few documents composed by Coronado that have been preserved in history.

I have done all that was possible in the service of Your Excellency to discover some region where our Catholic religion might be introduced and the rule of Spain imposed. But I found that things were very different from what Brother Marcos had reported, so I determined to explore this country in which I am now situated and which lies some five hundred miles to the northeast of Cibola.

Tiguex stands on a very fine river (the Rio Grande), but the villages which are built along its banks would not be worth colonizing with Spanish settlers, because they are so isolated and so very far from the ocean. It would be impossible to remain in contact with any such settlements.

This country is so extremely cold that it is almost impossible to remain here during the winter. Our men have the greatest difficulty in finding any firewood, and they utterly lack warm clothing. (Coronado does not mention that his soldiers had seized warm garments from the Indians.)

I am quite certain that in all this country there is neither gold nor silver. All I found were small villages whose Indian inhabitants, for the most part, do not trouble to plant the soil. They possess little except their leather tents or reed huts and live nomadic lives in company with the wandering herds of buffaloes.

That winter of 1542 was the worst period of all for Coronado's army. The men dared not stray too far from their camp for the Indians in the nearby pueblos remained sullen and unfriendly. Two soldiers, who incautiously went wandering around the countryside on their own, were never seen again. And as the ruthless hand of winter gripped the region, the insufficient food began to take its toll.

"We wear robes made of buffalo and our sleeping places are covered with buffalo skins," d'Arellano quipped with bitter humor. "Our hair and beards have grown long and shaggier than buffalo hides. We eat buffalo soup and buffalo stew and the marrow of buffalo bones. I grow scared of glancing in my metal mirror for fear that one day I shall see solemnly gazing back at me the countenance of yet another buffalo!"

Death walked through the Spanish camp that winter. Pneumonia took several lives. A sickness that might mave been typhoid destroyed others. At least one sentry was frozen to death as he stood on his midnight vigil.

Firewood was in such short supply that before the winter was over the Spaniards were forced to burn the roughhewn beams and wooden laths that formed much of the framework of the pueblo. Too late they realized that the walls promptly crumbled when the timber was removed. Snow drifted in through the apertures and melted in the comparative warmth of the interior of the building. Rivulets of water then penetrated to other rooms in which men were still living. This interminable dampness added much to the misery and discomfort of their dreary lives.

The winter passed and the sun began to rise higher above the southern horizon. By the end of March the temperature was becoming noticeably warmer and the snow was melting. But now a fresh and bitter argument arose among the Spaniards.

A number of the hidalgos were in favor of Coronado's plan to explore the country far to the north of Tiguex. Said Juan Jaramillo, a veteran officer who had endured more than his share of hardships and Indian fighting:

To equip myself for this expedition I was obliged to borrow heavy sums of money in Mexico City. Some of it went on a good horse, which, alas, is now doubtless being ridden by some rascal of an Indian. The rest of the money provided me with a much-needed wardrobe, which still lies aboard one of the two ships that deserted us. I have no doubt my creditors will eagerly line the roadside when I return to Mexico. If I possess neither gold nor silver with which to satisfy them, the *Juez de la Provincia* (State Judge) will give those villains leave to sell my house. Then I will be left both poor and homeless. A fortune may await us somewhere in the country our general plans to visit. Nothing but poverty and debts await me back in Mexico.

Those cavaliers who were luckily free of debt were hostile to the idea of spending another summer wandering through the heart of the country. They were eager to return to Mexico as soon as the necessary arrangements could be made. So were all those foot soldiers who had managed to survive the hardships of the past two years. The thought of returning to

Mexico with empty pockets did not worry them in the least. All their lives they had been accustomed to poverty; indeed their lives were the only thing they had to value.

Coronado accidentally provided a settlement of this argument. He rode out of the camp one day, accompanied by a cavalier named Pedro Maldonado, to practice hitting a target with his lance. He was mounted on his own good horse, but the saddle girth was rotten. While he was riding at full gallop this strap broke, the saddle slipped off the horse's back, and Coronado fell heavily to the ground. Maldonado's horse, which was racing along behind, accidentally struck Coronado on the head with one of its hooves. The general was picked up unconscious and carried to his bed.

For several days he lay, as Casteñada described it, "within the width of two fingers of death." For a full week he was unable to speak or recognize even his closest companions. At the end of two weeks he was somewhat recovered.

"Events are turning out as a fortune teller in Spain predicted long ago," murmured Coronado. "He declared that I would live to become a governor in a far-off country, but that a severe fall would put an end to my life. The governorship of Culiacán was a higher post than ever I dreamed of attaining, and I may yet die in this village of Tiguex."

But Coronado did not die. He began to make a slow recovery. Now, however, he changed his mind. He had spoken often of his wife while he lay sick, and he yearned to return to Mexico in order to see her again. As soon as he was able to walk he called a conference of his officers and informed them of his intention.

Cavaliers and foot soldiers were allowed to vote on the question, and the majority were in favor of a return to Mexico. Coronado, who was familiar with his fellow countrymen's peculiar memories, invited them to sign a statement to that effect.

With the growing warmth and sunshine of spring the argument soon started all over again. A number of the hidalgos changed their mind and declared that now they were in favor of making the northward trip. With some insolence they demanded that Coronado should hand them back the paper they had signed. Quite naturally he refused.

Matters then became somewhat disagreeable in the camp. The general, in order to avoid being pestered in this manner, kept to his lodging and declared he was in worse health than was actually the case. He placed a number of sentries on guard around the apartments he occupied, and even had one sentry on the balcony at night. Even so, however, someone managed to enter our commander's bedroom while he was asleep one night and forced open his private chest. But the document they sought was not there, for the general had placed it beneath his pillow.

Before setting off back to Mexico, Coronado made one last effort to bring off a worthwhile discovery. He sent one of his hidalgos, Captain Francisco de Barrio-Nuevo, and twenty soldiers in a northerly direction along the banks of the Rio Grande. At the same time he dispatched another officer to follow the river downstream.

Barrio-Nuevo traveled overland about 150 miles up the Rio Grande. The Indians he met during the first part of the journey were friendly, but when he reached the neighborhood of Sante Fe he began to encounter signs of hostility. The Indians fired a few arrows and managed to steal a Spanish horse. Then they deserted their handsome and well-built villages beside the river and retreated into the foothills of the Rocky Mountains. There they entered four strongly fortified villages, which the Spaniards wisely refrained from attacking.

In the abandoned settlements beside the Rio Grande Barrio-Nuevo found great quantities of food and also a number of large earthenware vessels, all of which were cleverly decorated with silver filigree. Where this silver came from was a mystery to the Spaniards. In the same region they discovered the most elaborate type of steam baths. These buildings stood on top of a dozen stone columns, each column being twelve feet high and six feet in circumference. The steam was created by heating stones in fires built on stone slabs inside the houses. When the stones were red-hot, quantities of water were poured over them.

As far as Barrio-Nuevo was concerned, this border country between New Mexico and Colorado was a somewhat arid and useless region. But one or two of the soldiers with him thought otherwise. "If these level valleys were irrigated," one said, "heavy crops of corn and wheat could be grown in the fertile soil. The cooler climate of this region would also be most favorable for the raising of cattle and sheep."

Once again it was those Spanish soldiers, the sons and grandsons of peasants who had always earned their living from the soil, whose judgment was correct. Although they were as eager as their officers to acquire gold, things such as soil, water, and grass always remained more real to them. With shrewd and experienced eyes they observed the slope of the hills, the sites for water catchment, and the rich upland meadows beside the mountain streams, where stock could graze and grow fat.

Captain Barrio-Nuevo, who knew nothing of farming and cared less, merely turned his back on the region and ordered the return march to Tiguex to begin.

Meanwhile, the second party of men had followed the course of the Rio Grande downstream to a distance of two hundred miles. They were no more impressed than Barrio-Nuevo with what they found.

They came to four very large Indian villages

whose inhabitants eagerly made friends with our men. At a considerable distance beyond these villages they reached a spot where the river disappears underground like the Guadiana River in Spain. But having orders to advance no farther to the south than two hundred miles, our party did not reach the spot where, according to the Indians, the river reappears in greater volume than at the point where it disappeared underground.

Thus ended Coronado's exploration in North America. Spring of the year 1543 was now passing into early summer, and the time had come to begin the homeward march to Mexico. Even as the army prepared for the journey, a missionary named Brother Luis decided to remain behind in Tiguex.

As the Spaniards filed out of the pueblo for the last time and turned their faces to the west, the lonely black-robed figure of Brother Luis watched them out of sight. He never returned to Mexico and no one learned what finally happened to him. It was rumored, however, that in later years he was killed by the vengeful natives of Cicuye.

The Indians made no effort to prevent the Spaniards from departing. They were probably overjoyed to see them go. Standing on rocky pinnacles, outlined against the pale blue of a cloudless sky, bronze-skinned and befeathered warriors stood gazing down on the moving column of horses, fluttering banners, and mail-clad men.

A few more horses disappeared during the first few nights, but then the other horses began to die in great numbers. The reason remained a mystery.

Between Tiguex and Cibola a very strange thing happened. Our horses, which were fat and in good condition in spite of their long and arduous service, began to die one after another. Altogether we lost more than thirty of them; two or three of them died nearly every day. Between Cibola and Culiacán still more of the animals perished. This was altogether remarkable and nothing like it had previously occurred during our whole outward journey.

The expedition rested for a couple of days in the pueblos of Cibola, where they bitterly recalled their disappointment on seeing these promised Seven Cities. A desert crossing now lay ahead and plentiful stocks of food and water had to be carried.

For some reason or other, the Sonora Indians refrained from making any attempt to destroy the Spaniards. Perhaps they thought they had achieved sufficient revenge by wiping out the settlement of San Hieronimo. The only living creatures seen on that wearisome crossing were desert lions in great numbers, wildcats, lynxes, and—in the occasional streams—innumerable otters. The Indians themselves remained entirely out of sight.

The Spaniards, being no longer burdened with mountainous baggage and tiresome mules and packhorses, were able to travel fast. Every man carried his possessions on his back. Lean and bearded, toughened by three years of primitive existence in the wilds, they were able to endure long daily marches, which, at the start of the expedition, would have caused most of them to collapse from fatigue by the wayside.

In September, 1543, they marched into the familiar town of San Miguel in Culiacán.

CHAPTER
TEN

**END
OF AN
EXPEDITION**

"Everyone believed," wrote Casteñada, "that his troubles were now at an end for we had reached a Christian country of which our general was the governor."

San Miguel was a picturesque little Indian

town of narrow, winding streets and adobe huts. Coronado's official residence, a Spanish fort, and the treasury were the only stone buildings—built by Spanish masons—that the town possessed. But there were plenty of wine taverns with cool interiors and even a busy marketplace where meat and fish and vegetables could be obtained without trouble.

These amenities quickly began to loosen the last shreds of discipline that had held Coronado's men together. For days on end they ate and drank riotously. They slept on cord-strung wooden pallets, which were infinitely more comfortable than a blanket spread on the hard soil of the prairies. Officers and men no longer intermingled, and each man went his own way.

The expedition had set out from Mexico City and Don Mendoza was still expecting its official return there. No expedition of any kind—not even an unsuccessful one—could be allowed to fade out of existence before it was officially disbanded. The return march to Mexico City would have to be performed.

Coronado made the mistake, for which no one can blame him, of remaining for two weeks at his home in Culiacán with his wife Beatrice and their little child. This long rest, however, caused his army to fall utterly apart.

Probably Coronado himself knew that he was delaying longer than he should have. He was a failure in the eyes of the Spanish government and, a shrewd and sensible man, he knew it. Trumpets were sounded, rich carpets unrolled, and distinguished honors made available only for those explorers who returned with plundered treasure to fill the greedy coffers of Spain.

Coronado had merely found and widely explored a vast new country of illimitable acres of virgin forest and rolling savanna. He had mapped unknown rivers, found passes through the high sierras, measured distances, and noted latitudes. But he had found neither gold nor silver.

The rulers of Spain, who lacked both imagination and foresight, never realized that navigable rivers, fertile soil, and ample supplies of timber for every human need represented the most precious wealth of any nation. In their greedy eyes a bloodstained jewel from some looted Indian temple was more valuable than a prosperous site for a ten-thousand acre homestead. In that respect the humble unknown soldiers who marched with Coronado across the future United States were wiser than their rulers.

At the end of the two weeks in Culiacán Coronado managed to round up most of his grumbling and discontented troops. Forming them into the semblance of a disciplined force, he continued his march along the coast to Campostella.

The autumn had arrived and seasonal torrential rains were turning the unsurfaced coastal roads into muddy trails. Desert rivers, which for the greater part of the year were merely dry and cactus-bordered arroyos, had now become flooded and dangerous torrents. Crocodiles in great numbers appeared in them as if from no-where. A wretched Spanish soldier was seized by one of these brutes and dragged away be-fore any of his companions could flounder to his assistance with drawn swords.

The incessant rain, the wet firewood, and the utter discomfort of soaked garments again brought the mood of the miserable troops to the stage of mutiny. By one's and two's they began to desert in every village they reached.

Of the sturdy and glittering force of 320 Spaniards, which had set out from Mexico City in 1540, less than 100 muddy, ragged, and pen-niless survivors returned at the end of 1543. Among them was faithful Pedro Casteñada de Nagera.

With unusual modesty for a Spanish hidalgo, Casteñada makes no mention in his diary of his own exploits during the entire three years. By

not a single word does he attempt to set himself above his companions, or to make any
reference to his own exertions and disappoint-
ments. All that one knows for certain of him is
that he was a man of great vision and understanding. Like the humble soldiers who crumbled soil between their fingers, he guessed
rightly that the future of North America lay
not in gold or silver, but in her earth and timber and water.

Casteñada at last reaches the end of his story.
One of his final entries reads:

Our general was very ill received by His Excellency the governor, but having carried out his orders in a most faithful manner, he was given his
discharge. The adventure cost Coronado his good
reputation in Mexico, and some time later he was
relieved of his position as governor of Culiacán
province.

Dismissal brought no hardship, and probably

little disappointment, to Coronado. He possessed sufficient wealth to continue living in comfortable circumstances. He had never seen eye to eye with the fanatical and unimaginative officials whom Spain sent out across the Atlantic Ocean to rule her empire in the New World. Accompanied by his wife and child, and surrounded by his beloved books and papers, Coronado built his own comfortable home in Culiacán, planted a spacious, flower-filled garden around it, and lived an obscure but peaceful and contented existence to the end of his days.

By the historians of Spain and Mexico he was soon forgotten. His name is featured only briefly in most accounts of the exploration of North America. It was not until 1805, however, that two American government explorers named Major Pike and Lieutenant Brown reached, during their respective journeys, much of the vast region that Coronado had explored more than 250 years before them.

Spain herself turned her back on North America. First de Soto, then de Vaca, and finally Coronado had all failed to find in that country the only kind of wealth her rulers understood. They had held in their grasp the greatest country of the world, but now they tossed it aside thoughtlessly without a trace of regret.

Having scorned the gift of North America, Spain soon proceeded to prove her inability to maintain the empire she had already won in the Caribbean. Her island plantations deteriorated. The enslaved Indians died off. Imported Negro labor proved expensive. When industrious Spanish peasant settlers should have been plowing the land and stringing their fences, a host of grandees and adventurers foolishly continued to drift across the mainland in every direction in an endless search for nations to plunder and mines to exploit.

And so it came about that in the end Spain was ousted by more vigorous nations, which swept aside her vainglorious claims to the "continent, islands, harbors, and waters of all America."

BIBLIOGRAPHY

Anonymous, *Don Coronado through Kansas*, Seneca, Kansas, Don Coronado Company, c. 1908

Catlin, G., *Letters & Notes on the North American Indians*, London, Tilt & Bogue, 1842

Gage, Thomas, *A New Survey of the West Indies*, printed in London, 1699

Higginson, Thomas W., *History of the United States*, New York, Harper Brothers, 1886

Lummis, C. F., *The Spanish Pioneers and the California Missions*, Chicago, McClurg, 1929

Pike, Major Z. M., *Voyage au Nouveau-Mexique*, privately printed in London, 1812

Ternaux-Compans, H., *Relation du Voyage de Cibola*, Paris, Arthus Bertrand, 1838

Vega, Garcilasso de la, *La Florida del Inca*, new edition, London, Thos. Nelson & Sons, Ltd., 1951

RONALD SYME spent his boyhood in New Zealand, sailing and hunting wild boar much of the time. At sixteen, he left school and went to sea in a Pacific cargo steamer, and for four years he traded between Australia, New Zealand, San Francisco, and the South Sea Islands. At eighteen, he began writing short stories, and in 1934 he left the sea to become a professional writer.

During World War II Mr. Syme served in the British Merchant Service as a gunner until he was transferred to the British Army Intelligence Corps because he spoke four foreign languages. He also fought with the Eighth Army in Africa and became a paratrooper during the Italian campaign.

Today Mr. Syme is a well-known author in both England and the United States. An insatiable voyager, he still continues to visit various portions of the globe, for research or pleasure. He once sailed 1660 miles in a twenty-ton schooner from New Zealand to Rarotonga in the Cook Islands, where he now lives.

NEVADA

UTAH

CALIFORNIA

Grand

Colorado River

Canyon

Painted
Desert

ARIZONA

Gila River

Black R.

PACIFIC
OCEAN

Gila Desert

Gila Cliff
Dwellings

Coronado
National
Memorial

Sonora River

GULF OF CALIFORNIA

OUTWARD JOURNEY ∙∙∙∙∙∙∙∙∙∙
HOMEWARD JOURNEY ─ ─ ─ ─

0   100   200   300 MILES